'What a gift Paul has brought to those ⟨…⟩ live with the ever-present danger of tr⟨…⟩ allows. Based on his own personal exp⟨…⟩ from scripture and a breadth of readin⟨…⟩ case for self-care. His healing message is liberating and timely. It is a call to learn how to work with God, not just for God. It is a summons to dare to believe "I too am more important than my ministry."'
Tony Horsfall, author of *Servant Ministry* (BRF, 2013)

'Paul Swann offers biblical insight alongside wisdom born of personal experience into an aspect of ministry to which many leaders fail to give sufficient attention – our own emotional and spiritual well-being. This is an honest and helpful book for all in, preparing for or considering church leadership.'
Emma Ineson, Principal, Trinity College Bristol

'As I read this timely book in order to endorse it, I realised that I could not rush it, and you will not be able to either. The pervading challenge of keeping the balance between what we give out and take in, spiritually, is an electrifying antidote to the intoxicating, yet crippling lure of productivity and personality-driven ministry. Through this written masterclass on how to care for your soul, Paul Swann has managed to distil lashings of ancient and contemporary wisdom, combine it with his own intensely personal story, and provide a precious recipe for how to get going, keep going and finish well – and not just in leadership and ministry, but life generally! I shall be recommending it widely as crucial reading for folk that I mentor and coach, who need to be constantly reminded that they are more important than their ministry.'
Paul Wilcox, mentor/coach and author of *Intentional Mentoring* (Instant Apostle, 2018)

'Paul has truly gifted us a book full of wisdom, insight, hope and encouragement. It's the fruit of his own journey and leadership story that he speaks of with honesty and courage. Paul invites us to discover the freedom of embracing our weakness, ministering in vulnerability, and letting what we do truly flow from who we are and whose we are. I am privileged to have followed in his footsteps here at All Saints, and even more so to have journeyed with him over the last few years and seen how God has worked in and through Paul in such powerful and beautiful ways. Any leader, of whatever kind, committed to going the distance and finishing their race must read this book, carefully and prayerfully.'
Rich Johnson, New Wine Chair of Regional Directors,
Regional Director for the South West and vicar of All Saints Worcester

The Bible Reading Fellowship
15 The Chambers, Vineyard
Abingdon OX14 3FE
brf.org.uk

The Bible Reading Fellowship (BRF) is a Registered Charity (233280)

ISBN 978 0 85746 651 8
First published 2018
10 9 8 7 6 5 4 3 2 1 0
All rights reserved

Acknowledgements
Unless otherwise stated, scripture quotations are taken from The Holy Bible, New
International Version (Anglicised edition) copyright © 1979, 1984, 2011 by Biblica.
Used by permission of Hodder & Stoughton Publishers, an Hachette UK company.
All rights reserved. 'NIV' is a registered trademark of Biblica. UK trademark number
1448790.

Scripture quotations marked MSG are taken from *The Message*, copyright © 1993,
1994, 1995, 1996, 2000, 2001, 2002 by Eugene H. Peterson. Used by permission of
NavPress. All rights reserved. Represented by Tyndale House Publishers, Inc.

Scripture quotations marked NRSV are taken from The New Revised Standard Version
of the Bible, Anglicised edition, copyright © 1989, 1995 by the Division of Christian
Education of the National Council of the Churches of Christ in the United States of
America. Used by permission. All rights reserved.

'Patient Trust' (page 31) is copyright © The Institute of Jesuit Sources and reproduced
with permission.

Extract from Common Worship: Services and Prayers for the Church of England
(page 42) and prayer (page 50) are copyright © The Archbishops' Council of the
Church of England, 1995, 1997 and are reproduced with permission.

'Let Your God Love You' (page 95) and 'Balance' (page 96) are copyright © Edwina
Gateley (**edwinagateley.com**) and are reproduced with permission.

Every effort has been made to trace and contact copyright owners for material used
in this resource. We apologise for any inadvertent omissions or errors, and would
ask those concerned to contact us so that full acknowledgement can be made in
the future.

A catalogue record for this book is available from the British Library

Printed and bound by CPI Group (UK) Ltd, Croydon CR0 4YY

You are more important than your MINISTRY

SUSTAINING LEADERSHIP

PAUL SWANN

This is for all who are on a journey of serving God and others in the hope that it may provide resources for the journey.

I could not have completed this without the help of many remarkable people, not least Viv, Tim, Peter and Chris who have travelled with me most closely. I am deeply thankful.

CONTENTS

FOREWORD

I have the utmost respect and admiration for Paul Swann and am delighted to commend his book wholeheartedly. It has been a privilege to share Paul's painful journey with him in a small way over the last ten years.

Here, Paul offers profoundly insightful as well as practically useful reflections on that journey as he tells a powerful story of descent into utter powerlessness. We are plunged headlong into the sudden and terrifying loss of physical and mental strength that Paul experienced in the midst of an exciting, creative and demanding ministry, a loss he characterises as 'disintegration'. His openness about his chronic fatigue syndrome and his arrival on 'Planet Fragile' provides moving evidence of the way he has learned the difficult, painful yet ultimately life-restoring need to embrace vulnerability. He then moves on to a detailed analysis of the factors, forces and, yes, people who can drive any leader beyond sustainability. Paul writes from a deeply personal perspective, but his honesty and beautiful prose enable the reader to identify with his experience and to recognise within themselves some of their own fragility and weaknesses, as it certainly did in my case.

In the second and third parts of the book, Paul offers some profound theological reflection on reintegration, as well as a host of practical measures towards beginning and maintaining that process. Woven all the way through is the conviction, borne out by his experience, that dependence on God is the only sure way to avoid the lures and snares of leadership and to discover true human identity. Paul draws on a vast range of authors from a variety of backgrounds – spiritual, theological, literary and cinematic. On every page you will find pearls of wisdom that provide stimulus for productive reflection, in addition to which Paul provides clear and challenging questions and points to ponder.

Those in positions of leadership in the church will find rich resources here to enable them to flourish. But this book is not just for them: it is for anyone with a lively interest in the dynamics and interactions of human community, and for anyone who seeks insights into the mystery of God. Paul's story is indeed a powerful account of powerlessness, and it is also more: it is an eloquent testimony to the God whose strength is made perfect in weakness, the God of resurrection.

John Inge, Bishop of Worcester
25 January 2018 (Feast of the conversion of St Paul)

INTRODUCTION

A chance meeting I have with a church leader catches him off guard, meaning he answers my 'How are you?' more truthfully than he intends. His face subconsciously relaxes from a forced smile into the more revealing weariness and disappointment which lie beneath his cheery countenance. His tale is a familiar, but nevertheless real and painful one of working himself into the ground in a context that is unresponsive and even hostile. When the time comes to move on, searching for a way to encourage him, I urge him to look after himself within that harsh environment, a suggestion which seems totally alien. I quote Parker Palmer: 'Self-care is never a selfish act – it is simply good stewardship of the only gift I have, the gift I was put on earth to offer to others.'[1] I see from the almost imperceptible softening of his eyes that this is an entirely new but hope-filled concept. At no point in his long, faithful ministry has anyone suggested to him that self-care is a good, even biblical, value. Worn into the ground, wondering how much longer he can keep going, he receives this word like parched and spent soil welcomes a drop of refreshing rain.

A vicar shares her frustration that recruiting volunteers is growing ever harder. She notices that people in her church have historically been so committed and loyal that to volunteer for any role has become tantamount to taking on a job for life. That has turned into the unspoken and unintended model for lay ministry. When faithful volunteers become too frail to continue, they step aside, exhausted and empty. Is it any wonder that those asked to fill the role dare not risk taking it on? Wisely, she is planning a teaching series on the nature of rest and self-care within the church before the next round of volunteer recruitment.

A young man was making visits to the elderly. All day he experienced sharp pains in his abdomen but still did not want to neglect the final two visits. Surreptitiously clutching his stomach, he spent an agonising hour trying to listen to the needs of the first couple, while fighting the pain within. On arriving at the next address, it was with enormous relief that he received no response and finally went home to rest. That was not a decision he felt able to make for himself. Within hours he had been diagnosed with acute appendicitis and was receiving emergency surgery. Even under intense physical pain, self-care was not in his vocabulary.

This is what this book is about. These are real stories (with contexts changed). Similar stories are repeated daily among countless church and ministry leaders, as well as helpers and volunteers, all seeking faithfully to serve God and his people. I write from deep personal experience which has birthed in me a passion for us to learn what it means to take good care of ourselves in ministry. All Christians involved in some form of service have to make hard decisions to find the balance between giving to others and looking after themselves. This book contains hard-learned insights and practical tools that we can make use of to ensure this remains a short-term experience, through which we can not only grow personally but also continue serving with faithfulness, creativity and joy. *Sustaining Leadership* is not a book about what to do as a leader. It is about how to be as a leader.

You may already be in the distressing place of feeling trapped in a pattern that has become unsustainable, caught between the desire to keep going and the real fear that to stay might be seriously damaging to you and to those around you. This story and the lessons that emerge from it are for you.

Even if you are currently sailing along in ministry full-time or part-time, paid or voluntary, my hope is that this book will help you to keep on that track and continue to serve the Lord with joy for many years to come.

We need to know that even in contexts that are responsive, challenges will come. David Runcorn has said, 'It is one of the most frequent areas of neglect – the care for the strong in our churches... Often the most tired, isolated and discouraged were not those who had experienced failure in their Christian lives... They were those whose strength had run out in the course of loving and faithful service.'[2]

This is what happened to me. I came to a full stop. One day I was in my bishop's study, as if in some eerily calm nightmare, hearing myself say these words:

I can't do this any more.

I didn't know what would happen after making such a risky confession. In the days which unfolded from there, everything was scrubbed from my to-do list and I was left staring at a sheet of paper that was blank except for this one thing: 'Take good care of yourself!' The only questions were 'Is it too late to start?' and 'Do I even know what that looks like?'

I'm still working out the answers to those questions, but I have found as I share my story that the changes I have made and the things I have learned about myself, God and ministry have been encouraging to others in their own life and ministry. Now I am privileged to be able to make this offering to 'all you who are weary and burdened' (Matthew 11:28).

DISINTEGRATION

1

ENCOUNTERING FRAGILITY

Beginnings

When I was seven years old, I desperately wanted an Action Man for Christmas. I nagged my parents relentlessly and, sure enough, on Christmas morning, there was the right-shaped gift under the tree. But as I eagerly ripped off the wrapping, I could see immediately that there was a problem. This wasn't Action Man, but Fighting Yank! No, I hadn't heard of him either. That initial disappointment deepened when I removed one of his boots for the first time. Not only did the boot come off but so did his foot. The toy was broken within the first few minutes, and I didn't play with it much after that.

Looking back, that was my first real encounter with fragility. I decided I didn't really like broken things very much. Although I grew to find a place in my heart for the broken people I met along the way, it was a long time before I would be comfortable with the brokenness I found within myself. In the end, it would take a major encounter with brokenness in my own life to move me closer to being at ease with fragility. It's not a subject with which we are very comfortable. Mark Oakley has said, 'We're very good at truth in the church but not so good at honesty.' And he warns against the wearing of masks, which 'if worn too long eat into the face so that you lose track of where one begins and the other ends'.[3]

This book will recount honestly how the presence of my own mask was revealed only when painfully stripped away. Only then could I commence my journey of discovering where the mask ended and my true self began.

Treasure in clay jars

We should not be surprised by our fragility. The apostle Paul speaks of it clearly in his imagery of carrying the treasure of Jesus 'in jars of clay to show that this all-surpassing power is from God and not from us. We are hard pressed on every side, but not crushed; perplexed, but not in despair; persecuted, but not abandoned; struck down, but not destroyed' (2 Corinthians 4:7–9). In this passage of unadorned reality and profound hope, Paul refers to the sort of fragile jars which were two a penny in his day. Common, everyday items that could easily be replaced if they were broken, they were often used as household lamps. It was the very fragility of the clay that allowed the light to shine through. They were so fragile that they are rarely found by archaeologists because most simply have not survived.

In this first section, I will describe my plunge into fragility. It's the story of how I found that peace comes not when we deny or even fight that, but when we embrace who we are. I want to share this because we can only start from where we are, but also in order to offer the sort of transparency that may help to shed some light on your fragility. As Sheila Cassidy says, 'More than anything I have learned that we are all frail people, vulnerable and wounded; it is just that some… are more clever at concealing it than others! And… the great joke is that it is OK to be frail… because that is the way the almighty God made people.'[4]

Our inspiration to honesty comes from Psalm 34:

> Never hide your feelings from him. When I was desperate, I called out, and God got me out of a tight spot… Is anyone crying for help?… If your heart is broken, you'll find God right there; if you're kicked in the gut, he'll help you catch your breath.
>
> PSALM 34:5b–6, 17a, 18 (MSG)

Arriving on Planet Fragile

My story of being kicked in the gut began in March 2005. I went to bed one evening exhausted, as I had many times before. I woke up the next day and found myself living on an alien planet. At first glance, everything looked familiar, but this planet had an accelerated rotational speed so that it was impossible to stop the bedroom spinning. Gravity was stronger, so the effort required to lift my head off the pillow was substantially increased. How could my limbs have become so heavy overnight? When I did get out of bed, I couldn't stand up.

The density of this strange planet exaggerated my fragility. Confidence-sucking black holes drew me into dark places. Wild whirlwinds of anxiety were liable to blow up at any moment. Soon, periods of drought blew in on hot, unforgiving winds, leaving the ground arid and fruitless.

My arrival here came as a complete shock. My journey had been going fine. University followed school and then I spent six years working in marketing and serving in my local church. In 1987, I trained for ordination before spending twelve demanding but fulfilling years in the urban Black Country of the West Midlands. In 2002, I moved to Worcester in response to God's call to plant a vibrant Anglican church there. It was brave and foolish, exciting and scary in equal parts. We started with no resources, but by God's grace we experienced rapid growth and soon had a viable and flourishing church. However, the investment of time and energy had been enormous and, at the very moment when things in the church were really taking off, my health plummeted in the opposite direction.

Initially thinking I had a 24-hour virus on that March morning, I crawled back into bed hoping that I'd be back to normal the next day. I could not have been more mistaken. The most significant consequence of the strong gravitational pull was extreme fatigue. Raising my hands above shoulder level was hard, as was undertaking simple tasks like having a shower, getting dressed or walking more than a few yards. Alongside the fatigue there was constant muscle pain, which was bearable during the day but exaggerated in the long hours of the night so that it became impossible to sleep, adding further to the fatigue.

And the hostility of this new environment was not merely physical; some atmospheric poison messed up my head too. I lost the ability to focus, so that I could not read more than a paragraph at a time. I struggled to hold a conversation for longer than a few minutes. In addition, someone had turned up the stimulus intensity so that light and sound were hard to cope with or even painful. My new planet's array of germs meant that my compromised immune system left me vulnerable to frequent and persistent infections. This unfriendly environment was a deeply isolating place to inhabit.

Some will quickly recognise this planet, but many medical people I encountered had never been there and some denied its existence. It would take a host of futile and invasive tests over a period of 18 months before I was diagnosed with the condition I had long suspected I had, most commonly known as myalgic encephalomyelitis (ME) or chronic fatigue syndrome (CFS).

Hitting the buffers

I spent three years trying to manage my health, including one extended break which lasted a full year. Feeling better, I returned to work in spring 2008 and continued to try to balance health and church. However, by the summer it became clear that this was not sustainable and, if I was to survive and the church to thrive, I needed to step down from leadership.

The stress of trying to keep going had brought me to breaking point. My confidence was so undermined that even walking into a room full of my supportive congregation felt unbearable. Finally came a week of painful yet grace-filled conversations with my bishop and church leaders, to whom I finally said, 'I can't do this any more. If I stop now there's a chance I might be able to be put back together again. If I don't, I'm not sure.'

Now came a host of questions: 'Will the flow of tears ever cease? What will happen next? How will we live? How will others respond? How can I let so many people down?'

Life on Planet Fragile

With my health at a low ebb, my energy levels minimal and my confidence in tatters, I and my family faced all the struggles that ensue from a loss of income and role for the main breadwinner. We gave up the house that went with the job, battled to find somewhere to live, and had to adjust to the change in responsibility, status and security.

This former apparently robust vessel had been placed under such extreme pressure that its true fragility had been exposed. I wanted to rewrite the apostle Paul's words into something more brutally honest: 'I was so hard pressed on every side that I was crushed; so perplexed that I reached the point of despair; feeling abandoned; struck down and facing destruction.'

After I stopped working, my health worsened for a while as my body was allowed to let go into its full brokenness, and I faded into a shadow existence, in which I became defined by illness itself. My first thought on waking was 'How am I today?' The activities of the day would be constrained by the extent of my energy. The world of the sick person is shrunk down to minimal size, like the mat of the paralysed man (Luke 5:17–26). Conversations with others revolve around the 'How are you?' question. This has to be asked, but it generates the pressure to respond with a positive answer in the face of the discomfort shown by others when that is not provided.

I echoed the psalmist's cry: 'I have become like broken pottery' (Psalm 31:12).

On Planet Fragile I found that it's not just that simple tasks become hard, and more demanding ones virtually impossible, but worse than that, even the things you love reposition themselves frustratingly beyond your grasp.

It is a desolate place. Life went from fullness of activity on Planet Busy to the vacuum of doing nothing. Occasionally I could stand the feeling of uselessness no more. Once I decided to contribute to life at home by defrosting the freezer. My wife came home from a long day in the office to find the job half done, and me sitting exhausted on the kitchen floor surrounded by rapidly defrosting food.

Some people handle suffering well and develop a sense of serenity. I am not one of those people! I became exasperated, frustrated and, finally, depressed. Those who had to spend the most time around me at that time will bear witness to the fact that I could be very difficult to live with.

The atmospheric pressure exposed more fault lines than I knew I had. Cracks in my faith, character, foundations and relationships were opened up for all to see. Shame and guilt were frequent visitors. Russ Parker speaks of a time of sickness: 'I felt guilty for not recovering. I felt a failure in succumbing to illness, and in not being able to do my work.'[5] This burden of guilt further strained my limited reserves of energy. As the effects of the illness began to impact those for whom I felt responsible – my wife and children, wider family and friends, the church itself – this guilt became, at times, unbearable.

Darkness descends

Sometimes these moments come and go, but when the fragility persists, an unrelenting darkness can fall, creating a place of absence more than presence. The God who I had known intimately for many years seemed to withdraw into the shadows just at the time when I needed him most. And that was probably the hardest loss of all. The Christian community has long spoken of 'the dark night of the soul'[6] as a very real experience. It's a time when God's people cry, 'How long, Lord? Will you forget me for ever? How long will you hide your face from me?' (Psalm 13:1).

And you can't rush this experience, however much you want to emerge on the other side. There are no words to express the density of the darkness or the intensity of the isolation. I could be outside on the brightest day but experience total darkness. I could be in the midst of well-loved company and feel utterly alone.

I identified with how Elijah felt when he sat under a bush and said to the Lord, 'I wish I were dead' (to paraphrase 1 Kings 19:4). It was not the thought of taking my own life that surfaced so much as the desire to not exist, to not have to bear life any longer as it had become. Arguing with God about this journey through the darkness and pleading for escape, I sensed him saying, 'The only way out of the valley is through the valley.'

I've told my story to set the scene for what follows and also to prompt your own risky exercise in honesty. My story is offered as permission to look your own fragility in the face.

Dare to offer God your experiences of fragility using these words inspired by Psalm 5:3: 'Every morning I lay out the broken pieces of my life on your altar and I wait in hope for you.'

Pause to reflect

- What sort of word is 'fragility' to you? Is it in your vocabulary?
- Take some time to recall an experience of encountering fragility.
- What are the characteristics of your planet?

2

EMERGING FROM FRAGILITY

Strength through struggle

A man observed a moth struggling out of its cocoon. In an attempt to help, he enlarged the opening with scissors. The moth emerged easily, but its wings were shrivelled. The struggle through that narrow opening serves to force fluid from the body into the wings. Sometimes it is the struggle itself which aids our metamorphosis into the people God wants us to be.

Novelist Haruki Murakami puts it this way: 'Once the storm is over you won't remember how you… managed to survive… But one thing is certain. When you come out of the storm you won't be the same person who walked in. That's what this storm's all about.'[7]

As I emerge from my cocoon, my storm, I am discovering that this encounter with fragility has been, after all, a fruitful one. It has been a place of discovery and growth rather than of destruction. Maybe it is not so surprising that Paul is able to see his own weakness not as a thorn to be extracted but as a gift to be received.

Richard Rohr says:

> When life is hard, we are primed to learn something absolutely central… The huge surprise of Christian revelation is that the place of the wound is the place of the greatest gift… [After the cross] the very worst things have the power to become the very best things. Henceforth, nothing can be a permanent dead end; everything is capable of new shape and meaning.[8]

Here are some of the surprising fruits I have noticed as I emerge from fragility.

New dependence upon God

The apostle Paul's testimony in the face of suffering was that God said to him, 'My grace is sufficient for you' (2 Corinthians 12:9). It is easy to say we depend on God but, in reality, we usually depend on self, performance, gifts or success. The removal or disabling of those alternatives forces us to a deeper trust in God alone. Eventually, even in the face of mystery that shatters our neat and tidy understanding of God, we can declare with Job, 'The Lord gave and the Lord has taken away; may the name of the Lord be praised' (Job 1:21).

Two-and-a-half years on from the sudden and devastating loss of her husband, my friend Caroline was able to say, 'When the bombs go off, our faith is wounded and our foundations are challenged. All you believe is exposed and laid bare… But the invitation in the delay is to believe anyway, despite the disappointment and circumstance.'[9]

It doesn't make sense and I know of no way to jump straight to the end of this journey. Suffering generates hard questions:

- Does God really love me?
- What do I truly believe?
- Who can I trust?
- What did I do wrong?

But the invitation is to the deeper trust that God's love for us is not connected to whether life is going well or badly.

We were blessed to have within our church the gifted writer Denise Inge. As she wrote her last book she battled inoperable cancer with joy-filled trust. At her funeral, her final journal entry was shared: 'I have nothing to offer God but my poverty. A broken body and a longing heart. And a state of complete dependency.'

New identity

As trust in God deepens, so also our identity as God's children is liberated from what we do for him. Like the returning prodigal, we come to our senses and throw our bedraggled selves upon the mercy of the Father. Henri Nouwen writes, 'For as long as you can remember, you have been a pleaser, depending on others to give you an identity. But now you are being asked to let go of all these self-made props and trust that God is enough for you.'[10]

I am learning that Broken, Failed, Exhausted Paul is as welcome in God's arms as was Together, Successful, Busy Paul – and maybe more so, because now I'm willing just to be there rather than to dare to think that I deserve to be there. This is a grace only discovered in the bankruptcy of our own resources running out. It is beautifully expressed by Clare of Assisi: 'Oh blessed poverty that gives eternal riches to those who love and embrace it.'[11]

New humility

Seeds of humility may sprout beautifully out of this time of being buried in the darkness of trials. Now we can no longer hide from the truth that we are fragile creatures. And this, in itself, helps us to understand how modest our place in the cosmos actually is.

This is what God sought to evoke in Job when he asked, 'Where were you when I laid the earth's foundation?' (Job 38:4). Humility brings us back to our naked condition, where we learn to be free from self-importance. False humility is talking ourselves down, so that others will think we are spiritual or build us up again. True humility is about being real. It is viewing ourselves as we really are, from God's perspective, and acting accordingly. This humility is rejuvenating, enriching and emboldening. Whereas humiliation leaves us paralysed and powerless, humility empowers us. Rabbi Jonathan Sacks declares that 'humility is one of the most expansive and life-enhancing of all virtues'.[12]

New perspective

After Elijah's greatest success, he ran away as far as he could, sat down under a bush and prayed that he might die. Later, he revealed his loss of perspective in complaining that he was the only one left fighting God's cause. In the exhaustion which can come in the aftermath of success as well as failure, he thought it was all about him. But God spoke in a still, small voice to make this a transformation experience. It wasn't completely about Elijah after all. There were 7,000 others on God's side; it didn't all depend upon him (1 Kings 19:1–18).

Eugene Peterson says, 'None of us is the leading character in the story of our lives. God is the larger context… in which all our stories are lived.'[13] This revelation is like the moment Copernicus worked out that the sun didn't revolve around the earth. One Sunday in church, I heard a still, small voice saying, 'It's not all about you.' This word was humbling to that part of me that liked being the centre of the universe, but it was actually really good news. I had lived believing that everything was my responsibility. Now I could just get on with being me. If you are going to become the best 'you' that you can be, you must first discover the real you as opposed to the fake you that you may have thought you had to be.

New community

Although there is isolation in suffering, it is also true that people in touch with their fragility experience the community of the wounded. The apostle Paul tells the Corinthian Christians how 'the God of all comfort… comforts us in all our troubles, so that we can comfort those in any trouble with the comfort we ourselves receive from God' (2 Corinthians 1:3–4).

Rabbi Kushner relates the tale of a woman who was overwhelmed by grief following the death of her son. A wise man advised her, 'Fetch me a mustard seed from a home that has never known sorrow. We will use it to drive out the sorrow from your life.' The woman went from house to house, asking if the home had known sorrow. Of course, each one had, and she comforted her hosts until eventually this ministering to others drove the sorrow from her own life. Henceforth her world was grounded in a new and mutual vulnerability.[14]

Chris Russell speaks of this: 'The world is changed for those who suffer because we find in this community of suffering a depth and a height and breadth of relating that we never knew.'[15] Living on the periphery helped me to discover a lot of people who I might not otherwise have noticed – and helped them to feel more able to connect with me too.

New healing

The place of pain can also become a place of healing. At first, the experience of God touching me at the points of my weakness was a mystery. I have come to realise that his love is such that, while I am often content with my failings, God is committed to helping me grow into his likeness.

It's as if we each carry a weighty rucksack that we fail to notice, because we have enough strength to carry it and enough busyness to be distracted from it. Then circumstances bring it to our attention and force us to begin to deal with what we have been carrying.

It has taken me a long time and a considerable amount of professional help to start emptying my rucksack so that I now carry a lighter load. God's not finished with me yet, and a key part of the healing is to accept who we are in our weakness. Daring to shed the outer layers of protection we have assembled along the way, we get in touch with the clay-pot fragility of which the apostle Paul writes to the gifted and strong Corinthian church.

By the grace of God, this painful descent enables many to speak tentatively of the transforming power of that path. It is often when people have lost their foundation and then experienced God upholding them that they come out even more alive, and certainly more real, on the other side.

New maturity

Within the many variations of God's purpose for our individual lives, they all have in common the same ultimate destination: for us to be conformed to the image of Jesus. I don't believe God deliberately makes our lives miserable to teach us lessons, but I do believe God is big enough to use even the worst of things to move us from where we are to the place he would have us be.

Sometimes this process takes many years. Mike Bickle reflects on the maturity formed in Moses: 'The first forty years was gaining strength, then the second forty years was for him to lose strength; to become weak, in order that he might become the person God needed him to be to lead his people to freedom.'[16] Much has been made in the media of the challenging upbringing Archbishop Justin Welby experienced with his alcoholic father. Welby says, 'At the time, it felt horrible. Now it feels hugely valuable. God doesn't waste stuff.'[17]

I am truly grateful for the many people who have prayed for my healing over the years. I am much better physically now than I was, but I have also grown in many ways. And because of that I am grateful for the journey.

New intimacy

Jacob's life-changing encounter with God involved a dream in which he wrestled all night with God (Genesis 32:22–32). Wrestling with God contributes to his transforming work because, in that battle, you literally get to grips with him. And unexpectedly out of the struggle comes intimacy. But then the image of wrestling is close to that of embracing. I love that Jacob gave his wrestling ring the name Peniel – the place I got face-to-face with God.

I long for deeper intimacy with God, but in those years when things went smoothly, greater intimacy often seemed unattainable. However, I have found that there's no distance in wrestling! You experience the grip of your combatant and hang on with your own; you feel hot breath from heaving lungs; you hear each other's hearts pounding. You are bound to emerge different. You may walk away with a limp, but you will have also been closer to God than ever before.

Richard Rohr says: 'Darkness draws you to know God's presence beyond what thought, imagination, or sensory feeling can comprehend. God is calling you into deeper and closer intimacy, beyond anything you could achieve… closer than you could even dream.'[18]

There's a powerful phrase in the intimate poetry of the Song of Solomon. It speaks of those struggling to walk after journeying through the desert: 'Who is this coming up from the wilderness leaning on her beloved?' (Song of Solomon 8:5). Transformation comes as we learn a new way of walking that is about the right kind of leaning – a humble dependence that is all about Jesus and nothing about us. And the one upon whom we lean is 'our beloved'. The experience will take us to a new place of intimacy in which we know the fullness of God's love for us through the very necessity of having to lean on him.

Pause to reflect

- Are you encouraged that the downward path can lead to a new place of deeper intimacy with God?
- What has been your own experience of transformation through suffering?
- Make this poem by Pierre Teilhard de Chardin (1881–1955) your prayer:

Patient Trust

Above all, trust in the slow work of God.
We are quite naturally impatient in everything
to reach the end without delay.
We should like to skip the intermediate stages.
We are impatient of being on the way to something
unknown, something new.
And yet it is the law of all progress
that it is made by passing through
some stages of instability –
and that it may take a very long time.

And so I think it is with you;
your ideas mature gradually – let them grow,
let them shape themselves, without undue haste.
Don't try to force them on,
as though you could be today what time
(that is to say, grace and circumstances
acting on your own good will)
will make of you tomorrow.

Only God could say what this new spirit
gradually forming within you will be.
Give Our Lord the benefit of believing
that his hand is leading you,
and accept the anxiety of feeling yourself
in suspense and incomplete.[19]

3

EMBRACING FRAGILITY

Evangelist J. John jokes that the church can get rather hung up on titles that promote our status: 'The church is full of titles – Revd, Very Revd, even some people are given the title Venerable. Well my title is Vulnerable. I'm Vulnerable.'[20]

This is a title I am learning not only to accept but also to embrace, initially as an enforced consequence of my journey but increasingly as a conviction for a way of being. The leadership I am looking to sustain is one informed and shaped by this journey into fragility.

It begins with weakness, because through weakness we cannot do what we long to do and we find ourselves doing what we do not want to do. And because that is the human experience, we also encounter brokenness. That is what happens to us when we suffer the damage that is a consequence of our own and others' weakness. Broken people are fragile and the interplay between fragility and brokenness means both are reinforced. So it is natural that we find failure in our lives, because weak, broken and fragile people make mistakes and react inappropriately to people and circumstances.

Where does vulnerability come into this? Vulnerability is about the choice to no longer hide behind a mask of protection, but to let our wounds show. We dare to say, 'I'm weak. I'm broken. I'm fragile. I've failed. But I'm still me and I'm still loved.' Something beautiful happens when we risk making this choice. The negative cycle of destruction that can surround these words is broken and new roads are opened up, new connections are made, new possibilities emerge. The kingdom of God is at hand!

Of course, vulnerability is still scary. Actor Andrew Garfield describes meeting God through intense vulnerability. Approaching his first post-drama-school performance, he panicked: 'I've never felt so much terror, like mortal dread, not-enough-ness, self-doubt. Terror at revealing and offering my heart. Exposing myself.' To offer ministry is also to go to a place of exposure with no place to hide. To calm his nerves Garfield went for a walk and he found himself praying for help. Then he heard a street performer singing, and the imperfection of the performance struck home. 'His willingness to be vulnerable changed my life… literally the clouds parted and the sun came out and shone on me, and this guy and I were just weeping uncontrollably. And it was like God was grabbing me by the scruff of the neck and saying, "You've been thinking that if you go on stage you're going to die. But actually, if you don't you're going to die."'[21]

Like the prophet Jeremiah, we have times when we try to deny our calling (Jeremiah 1:6), but we also know that to actually do so is not an option. If it is being seen in our imperfection that terrifies us, it is being held in our vulnerability that will redeem us. That is the invulnerability of living in vulnerability.

The courage of vulnerability

John Holmes was invited to speak about the new life experienced in his inner-city parish, but a divisive leadership crisis had left him feeling worthless. He explained to the organisers, 'I have nothing to offer you but my weakness.' They responded, 'Well, offer us that then.' They explained that in prayer that morning, one of them had seen a picture of a broken priest's wafer being offered to God in the Eucharist. And God was saying, 'Offer your brokenness to me, and I will use it.'[22]

This is what happens when we take the risk of embracing fragility by choosing to be vulnerable. We allow our wounds to show, as Jesus did in his resurrection appearances. We decide to take the road of acknowledging imperfection rather than heading down so many cul-de-sacs of trying to appear strong or in control. We dare to believe that it is okay to be who we are in our brokenness.

Brené Brown speaks of this in her book *The Gifts of Imperfection*: 'Wholehearted living is about engaging in our lives from a place of worthiness. It means cultivating the courage… to wake up in the morning and think, "No matter what gets done and how much is left undone, I am enough."' Brown uses the word 'courage' not to mean heroism but 'to speak one's mind by telling all one's heart', which is the sense of its Latin root. That will include totally countercultural things like:

- asking for help (even if you are a man who needs directions)
- admitting fear (even among our peers or superiors)
- showing our emotions (both joy and sadness)
- sharing stories of imperfection (in contrast to tales of our successes).

Taking courage to be vulnerable is a conscious choice of how we want to live – to show up and be real, letting our true selves be seen. It's hard to take these risks, especially in our often harsh and very public world, but those who do so find that this courage has a ripple effect. As Brown says, 'Every time we choose courage, we make everyone around us a little better and the world a little braver.'[23]

In a beautiful expression of vulnerability, our church staff team recently risked sharing the lie about themselves that they found hardest to resist. Each of these gifted individuals shared their temptation to give in to feelings of failure, lack of self-worth and low confidence. It was a privilege to then share with one another in prayer, confirming the truth of who we are as God's children.

In the end, the greatest gift you can be to the people you serve is the real you. A priest was leaving the congregation where she had ministered for a number of years. One farewell comment from a new

Christian stood out from the rest for its wisdom: 'Whatever happens, please keep on being you!'

E.E. Cummings wrote, 'To be nobody-but-yourself in a world which is doing its best, night and day, to make you everybody-but-yourself means to fight the hardest battle which any human being can fight.'[24]

Some people may struggle to understand why we choose vulnerability. It is threatening to those who have become so used to hiding that they no longer know who they are. Practising authenticity can feel like a daunting choice. It's risky to put your true self out in the world; that's why it takes courage. But the alternative is to hide from the world the true self God has made. Konstantin Stanislavski, the man behind method acting, said, 'The person you are is a thousand times more interesting than the best actor you could hope to be.'[25]

While some may resist our vulnerability, many others will be drawn in and inspired by our willingness to be real. Here's the experience of Joe Vorstermans, from L'Arche community:

> I would give a gospel reflection and hope that my words gave nourishment to the community… Some years later, a former assistant wanted me to know how important my reflections had been for her. 'I especially remember one evening when you stood up and said, "It has been a hard week for all of us and I am very tired and tonight I have nothing to share," and then you sat down! That night I really felt that you were one of us.'[26]

In 2016, I did something quite remarkable for me: I ran the Worcester 10K. My journey towards that achievement began the previous year when I went to support a friend taking part. To be honest, I was more interested in the shared breakfast afterwards, but I watched the race and got drawn in.

But who drew me in? Not the elite athletes who sped past first. I knew there was no way I could compete with them. Not even my friend inspired me really. He's well built for running and takes it very seriously. The people who inspired me were the older runners, those who were a little overweight, the very young participants – and the clearly never-done-this-before people! As I watched them jog, walk and limp their way around the course I thought, 'If they can do that, perhaps I can too.' So I began to train and, the following year, I completed the course at my own pace. Perhaps as I did so, someone thought, 'Well if he can do it then perhaps I can too.'

When we promote our success stories and hide our failures we inhibit others from stepping out and trying something new for the kingdom of God. Jean Vanier says, 'I am struck by how sharing our weakness and difficulties is more nourishing to others than sharing our qualities and successes.'[27]

Pause to reflect

- What would it mean for you to risk saying, 'I have nothing to offer you but my weakness'?
- Is there anywhere you feel safe enough to do that?
- Have you any experiences of inspiring or being inspired by an encounter with weakness?

Wheat or weed

We often do not know what within us is weak and what is strong. We are more complex than these black-and-white categories. When Jesus was asked if weeds growing among wheat should be pulled out, his response was to let them grow together until the harvest, when God will differentiate between wheat and weeds (Matthew 13:28–30). It is not our task to figure out that messy combination of wheat and weed that lies within. As Martin Luther put it, we are 'simultaneously saint and sinner'.[28] Accepting this reality, and then living with it, takes a lot more patience, compassion, forgiveness and love than aiming for some illusory perfection that blinds us to our own faults. Acknowledging both the wheat and weeds keeps us from both thinking too highly of ourselves and dismissing ourselves (or those around us) as terrible.

The trouble with needing perfection to be happy with ourselves is that we then have either to blind ourselves to our own failings (and deny the weeds) or to give up in discouragement (and deny the wheat). It takes uncommon humility to carry both the dark and the light side of things. Perhaps the only true perfection is the honest acceptance of our imperfection. This is precisely what God can help us do. As Joseph Cooke says, 'Grace is the face love wears when it meets our imperfection.'[29]

This is a rediscovery of something learned long ago by the desert fathers and mothers. Rowan Williams recounts John the Dwarf saying, 'We have put aside the easy burden, which is self-accusation, and weighed ourselves down with the heavy one, self-justification.'[30] Williams pleads with his fellow Christians to abandon self-justification, which tells only their best stories and shows only their best side. That becomes a heavy and unending burden. The alternative, 'self-accusation', is to look our fallible self in the eye and be honest with others about what we see. In the end, honesty about our failings is the lighter burden because we believe that the burden is already known and accepted by God's mercy. We do not have to create, sustain and save ourselves. God has done, is doing and will do all.

By taking this route, we choose to allow our best-loved pictures of ourselves to die and to live without their protection. Of course, it can feel like hell, but the real hell is never to be able to rest from the labours of self-defence. Gradually, we come to see this way as a deliverance and understand how sages such as the desert fathers and mothers could combine relentless penance with confidence and compassion.

Embracing fragility, and living with the vulnerability that brings, occurs as we are coaxed into risking honesty by the confidence that God both forgives and heals. It enables us to continue our journey from right where we are, which after all is the only place we can start.

This could be revolutionary for the church. Rowan Williams asks this searching question:

> Can the church become a community where it is possible to engage each other in this kind of quest for truth of oneself without... being condemned for not having an acceptable spiritual life?[31]

For leaders, the uncomfortable reality is that this type of community will only emerge when we set the tone and begin with our own choice to live in vulnerability. We need to model a community in which maturity is defined by freedom for people to be who they really are. The saint shouldn't be someone who makes us think, 'That's too hard for me', but someone who makes us think, 'How astonishing! Human lives can be like that.'

The F-word – failure

We all have failure somewhere in our life. Even those who appear to be strong often are just doing a good job of covering their weaknesses. This is our instinctive response to the unwelcome F-word. Over the years, I have developed an ability to appear relaxed in public ministry. The reality is that I am like my near namesake, the swan, gliding along with feet paddling furiously under the water's surface. Recently, as I prepared to speak with an apparently calm exterior, my fitness tracker revealed my heart rate was racing at 100 bpm. Costica Bradatan writes:

> Failure is like original sin in the biblical narrative: everyone has it... we are all born to fail, we practice failure for as long as we

live, and pass it on to others… For all its universality, however, failure is under-studied… It's as if even the idea of looking at failure more closely makes us uneasy; we don't want to touch it for fear of contagion.[32]

Initially, when forced to admit that I could no longer lead the church, I was haunted by the spectre of this word 'failure'. Many sought to reassure me that I was not a failure and that illness was not my fault. I appreciated these attempts to exorcise the failure ghost, but in the end they did not get through to my core. The more people reassure you that you are not a failure, the more like a failure you feel. In any case, I did fail. There were mitigating factors and I had given of my best, but in the end the way to freedom came not in denial but in acceptance. Yes, I failed; but that does not change who I am or how much God loves me. Neither does it change God's ability to continue the life and growth of the church without me.

Now, instead of living with people's well-meant words, I can face the truth and move on, as much loved by God as I was when apparently on the crest of a wave – and more deeply aware of this too. I am now attempting to walk with this new courage to simply be who I am, without pretence. I have arrived here with great resistance, and I still take many detours along the way. But what liberty it is to discover that we can embrace our fragility and even failure.

In the book *Chasing Francis*, Brother Thomas speaks to the central character, who faces a ministry crisis:

> Everywhere I go, people… tell me about their… failures. You'll never be able to speak into their souls unless you speak the truth about your own wounds… All ministry begins at the ragged edges of our own pain… Tell your story with all its shadows, so people can understand their own. They want a leader who's authentic, someone trying to figure out how to follow the Lord Jesus in the joy and wreckage of life.[33]

Let's be honest – we have not been very good at this in the church. Perhaps this is especially so in the evangelical and charismatic world that I inhabit. We tend to prefer order, certitude and theological 'answers' for everything, rather than to live with mystery.

The first summer that I was ill, I took a break in the hope of recovery. When I returned, I felt an expectation to announce my healing. After all that's what we were praying for, and we were experiencing such dynamism in our church life that anything seemed possible. It was tempting to fake something. Instead I announced that I was no better than before. I then asked, 'Who else has a prayer which remains unanswered?' Of course, there were many hands up. We spent time praying for those living in the mystery of waiting for God in the gap between Good Friday and Easter Sunday. The continued presence of a chronically ill leader in an apparently successful church became a reminder of the now and not yet of the kingdom. Richard Rohr writes:

> Grace is found in the depths... And we know that the only 'deadly sin' is to swim on the surface of things, where we never see, find or desire God. *Thus, we must not be afraid of falling, failing, going 'down'.*[34]

Pause to reflect

- How comfortable are you with using the word 'failure'?
- How can we make our churches ones in which failure is not taboo?

The way God intends it to be

Embracing weakness is not simply about feeling better about our failure. True freedom comes when we move into line with the way God always intended things to be. A theology of power and plenty in material terms has no place in the scriptures; a theology of weakness and failure runs all the way through God's story.

In the beginning, we have the theological imagery of God forming Adam from the clay of the earth (Genesis 2:7). Then humanity falls prey to temptation, unable to resist the lies of the serpent, the appeal of the forbidden fruit or the desire for independence (Genesis 3). Adam and Eve's descendants follow in these familiar footsteps.

The stories of every Bible hero contain many more accounts of failure than of success. Abraham is revered for his extraordinary faith (Genesis 15:6), but also made decisions based on fear and impatience. Jacob carried his father's blessing only because he was a schemer. Moses was a great leader, yet he lacked confidence and once displayed such violent anger that he committed murder (Exodus 2:11–12). The stories go on, as the Bible writers make no attempt to hide these very visible weaknesses and failures among key players. I wonder why we find it so hard to do the same.

Alongside this comes God's tendency to choose the younger brother, the smallest tribe, the unexpected outsider and the externally unattractive. We might ask, 'What on earth was God thinking? Why did he pick such dubious characters to do his work? And why does he still seem to do the same?'

It certainly isn't because God is fooled in all this. Psalm 103 praises God's compassionate character, but also reveals that God knows exactly what he is taking on when he partners with us, 'for he knows how we are formed, he remembers that we are dust' (v. 14). We may be surprised, disappointed or discouraged by our own and others' failures, but God is never surprised and is always ready to respond with compassion because he remembers the moment when he made us out of dust and, drawing close, breathed his life into our nostrils.

The child in a manger

It is no mistake that God calls the broken to ministry. Sorry if you thought you were called because of your strengths; it is unlikely to work that way round. As Brennan Manning writes:

> One of the stunning lessons of the Bible is God's free use of fragile human beings to accomplish his purpose. He does not always choose the devout or even the emotionally well balanced. The Holy Spirit is the bearer of gifts and these gifts are sometimes lavished in peculiar places.[35]

The incarnation reinforces God's preference for vulnerability. Jesus entered the human experience of weakness in every way except for sin. God came to us in the riskiest way possible – conceived by the power of the Holy Spirit to grow in Mary's womb before being born in humble surroundings. One Christmas prayer includes this beautiful petition: 'As your living Word, eternal in heaven, assumed the frailty of our mortal flesh, may the light of your love be born in us to fill our hearts with joy.'[36]

This nativity reveals a weakness so powerful it transforms the universe. Angels announce to shepherds that the proof this is the Saviour will be their discovery of the baby lying in a manger. Paula Gooder says, 'The birth narratives are about the mind-blowing, brain-boggling truth that the God who shaped the universe into existence was prepared to be born as a tiny, vulnerable baby. This God chose a ludicrously risky means of redeeming the world he loved so much.'[37]

In this way, Jesus reveals to us truths that go to the heart of God's nature as Trinity. Human strength is about self-sufficiency and holding on. God's 'weakness' encompasses interdependence and letting go. God's mystery rests in mutuality: three 'persons' perfectly handing over everything, emptying themselves out, and then fully receiving what has been handed over.

The Greek for this, *perichoresis*, describes this mutually interdependent giving and receiving as so delicate and beautiful that it becomes a sacred dance. Indeed, this is the root of our word choreography. Richard Rohr writes, 'We like control; God, it seems, loves vulnerability. In fact, if Jesus is the image of God, then God is much better described as "Absolute Vulnerability Between Three" than "Almighty One".'[38]

The 2006 film *Children of Men* (dir. Alfonso Cuarón) portrays a dystopian future in which, with the failure of human fertility, the dying human race has descended into chaos. The character Theo has to escort a young refugee, Kee, to safety. She is indeed the key to the future because she is pregnant. She therefore carries within her salvation for humankind, if she can survive the battle raging between violently competing forces. Finally, she gives birth in a refugee camp and there follows a deeply moving illustration of the power of a newborn baby.

As Theo, Kee and her baby navigate the battlefield, soldiers catch a glimpse of them, and for a few moments this tiny infant has the power to still weapons and even cause soldiers to bow down in awe and wonder. It is only for a moment, but the image is poignant nevertheless. It is the image of our powerful God who makes himself small for our sake.

Suffering servant

As Isaiah prophesied of the suffering servant (Isaiah 53), Jesus' story continued as it began. The Word of God learned to talk. He had to practice walking on solid ground before he could consider walking on water. He faced every trial and temptation known to humanity; he experienced what it was like to be let down by friends, to feel hot and tired in the heat of the day, to get hungry and thirsty, to feel joy, sadness, pain, misunderstanding, anger and disappointment.

Jesus knew what it was to pray with blood-sweating desperation to the Father for the most unwelcome of cups to pass from him (Luke 22:39–44). And he knew what it was to be betrayed, abandoned, falsely accused, tortured and then executed in the most inhumane way known to man. Hanging on a cross, Jesus experienced the weight of the world's brokenness and sin, and what it was like to feel forsaken by his Father (Matthew 27:45–46). Laid in a borrowed tomb, Jesus seemed to have ended his whole mission in embarrassing failure. Henri Nouwen writes:

> Jesus invites us to embrace our brokenness as he embraced the cross and live it as part of our mission. He asks us not to reject our brokenness as a curse from God... but to accept it and put it under God's blessing for our purification and sanctification. Thus our brokenness can become a gateway to new life.[39]

We don't come to God by doing it right. We more often come to God by getting it wrong. Our failures and wounds lead us to total reliance upon God. Thérèse of Lisieux delighted in this truth, which she called her 'Little Way,' a way described as 'the willingness to be the person God calls you to be'.[40]

Choosing weakness

When we see this, we wonder why we continue to seek the way of power, strength and control. We know that this is not who God is or what God is looking for. When Jesus recruited a team to accompany him and ultimately lead the emerging Christian community, he picked the ordinary, the fallible, the unexpected and the excluded. He entrusted the first testimony of his resurrection to a woman of dubious background. When he commissioned his disciples (John 20:20–22), he showed them his wounded hands and side, and said, 'As the Father has sent me, I am sending you' (v. 21). Then Jesus breathed on them, evoking the first creation and foreshadowing the coming of the Holy Spirit. The manner of our sending, our mission, is always about the power of the Holy Spirit inhabiting human flesh which bears the wounds of our own brokenness along with the wounds which have been inflicted upon us.

New message, new methods

Jesus' disciples learnt what it meant to follow him through failed fishing trips, under-catered picnics and abortive exorcisms. They began to learn that there was a new way of being, where they got to be with Jesus but didn't have to pretend about what they could and couldn't do. None of their discipleship training appeared to focus on capability. Jesus wants those who follow him to know what it means to be led to the place of powerlessness, which invites us to do the riskiest thing of all – to admit our lack and put our trust in him; to see what happens next to our loaves and fish. Larry Crabb says:

> Brokenness is simply the release of spiritual power. It only happens through brokenness – the most underrated virtue in the Christian community today. Strength is not a virtue to be cultivated. It is a reality to be released. It gets released over the course of your lifetime as brokenness becomes more complete.[41]

Later, when the good news of Jesus was shared beyond the confines of Judaism, God selected Saul, the former zealous opponent of 'The Way', as his chosen messenger. Saul understood that the way of Jesus represented a whole new way of ministering that was about becoming empty not filling up; preferring the other rather than self; letting go of power and status not grasping them; choosing the downward path of servanthood and letting God do the lifting up. And to choose this even if to do so required an obedience that took him all the way to a cross-like place of exposure and brokenness.

Taking the name Paul ('the small one'), he developed this ministry of servant-hearted vulnerability in stark contrast to the achievement-driven, qualification-requiring, rule-keeping, heritage-demanding faith in which he previously was immersed. Now he could operate with integrity and honesty about the spiritual blindness that had led him to persecute the faith; his temperamental weaknesses that made him a slave to sin; and, finally, that mysterious thorn in the flesh that enabled him to find his strength in God alone.

And so, in contrast to many of our models of training, much of our practice and many of our testimonies, we discover this kingdom paradox: to focus on being strong might prevent God's power from being seen in our weakness. To avoid failure may inhibit God's greater purpose. It seems we grow spiritually much more by doing it wrong than by doing it right. Richard Rohr again: 'What a clever place for God to hide holiness, so that only the humble and earnest will find it!'[42]

On retreat, spending time with Paul's passage on his thorn (2 Corinthians 12:7–10), I wrote my own version of that testimony:

> In order to help me walk through life on a humbler and more trusting path, I was given a thorn in the flesh to wrestle with. I became afflicted by an illness which stripped me of capacity and security and this colluded with the accusing voice taunting me with lies about unworthiness – a voice I could no longer silence with furious activity or impressive achievements. Many times, I pleaded with God to heal me. But he said, 'My grace is sufficient for you. This weakness is your invitation to discover that I am enough and that you are okay. Your brokenness is not a hindrance to me working as powerfully as I choose. Return to that truth often, and rest in it.'

> So now this is how I am learning to live. With my focus on the gift of grace, being transparent about who I am in all my weakness so that Christ in me can shine through the cracks. Now, when challenges come, or setbacks, or hurtful words – even when things fall apart – I hold on to this joy because this

very experience of weakness in me creates the space for God to be powerfully at work.

I am finding, gradually, that this message of weakness at the core of the kingdom is not bad news but good. It is not paralysing but liberating. Brené Brown writes:

> Vulnerability is the birthplace of love, belonging, joy, courage, empathy, and creativity. It is the source of hope, empathy, accountability, and authenticity. If we want greater clarity in our purpose or deeper and more meaningful spiritual lives, vulnerability is the path.[43]

There is welcome and compassion and understanding for us in our weakness.

> For we do not have a high priest who is unable to feel sympathy for our weaknesses, but we have one who has been tempted in every way, just as we are – yet he did not sin. Let us then approach God's throne of grace with confidence, so that we may receive mercy and find grace to help us in our time of need.
> HEBREWS 4:15–16

Nothing is required of you

In the stillness of retreat, I received an extraordinary insight into what this place of gracious freedom looks like. On the first morning, I walked out into the beautiful gardens and it dawned upon me that instead of the day beginning with a list of tasks to be accomplished, the decks had been cleared. The diary was empty for the next eight days. This phrase resounded in my mind: 'Nothing is required of you.' As I repeated this phrase over and over, a loud exclamation emerged from deep within. It was somewhere between an hysterical laugh, a poignant sob and a long sigh of relief. Thank goodness I had the garden to myself at the time.

Nothing is required of you.

The knowledge of that truth holding fast for eight days brought such relief that I thought I would explode with joy. I realised that I had been living with a distorted sense of responsibility, not just for the weeks prior to the retreat and not just about work, but for years and about all aspects of my life. I was bearing a burden I no longer needed to carry.

As the startling light of grace-filled truth revealed this ugly and damaging distortion for what it was, I realised that God's invitation was to live with that freedom not merely for eight days' retreat from the world, but for the remaining days of my life in the midst of the world. And that would be grace and freedom indeed.

A 'nothing is required of you' starting point leads to a different way of approaching the things we feel are demanded of us. We will still have to-do lists, but we can approach them with freedom and flexibility, because nothing is required of you to be who you are. Instead of everything being urgent and identity-defining, some things can wait, some things can be passed on and some things can even be done less than perfectly or left undone, with priority being given to that which most needs to be done.

Brennan Manning says, 'The mature Christians I have met along the way are those who have failed and have learned to live gracefully with their failure.'[44] And that greater degree of graciousness with ourselves will, of course, flow over into the lives of the imperfect people we encounter along the way.

This is the leadership I am describing in this book. It is clay-jar leadership. That is the only way to lead, because each of us holds the treasure of Jesus in our own clay jar (2 Corinthians 4:7). There is no exemption for leaders. Paul uses this image with his Corinthian friends because they know the difference between their famed black-glazed pottery and the cheap pots used as lamps. Paul's weaknesses are like that poor-quality clay: people are not to look at Paul and be impressed; rather they are to look through his weaknesses to see God's light.

Kintsugi is a Japanese practice of mending broken pots with gold or other precious metals so that the resulting pot is more beautiful than the one that broke. Someone recently showed me a pot she had made for her mother from one her brother had carelessly broken. She used the art of *kintsugi* to put the pot back together, and I could see how this offering was even more beautiful as a result of being carefully reconstructed with lines of gold.

As Christians, and as leaders, we are not called to be perfect. We are called to be who we are with all our imperfections, knowing that God's glory will shine through those cracks into the world around us and that the gold of God's love will mend our brokenness into something far more beautiful than it was before.

Martin Scorsese's beautiful film *Hugo* (2011) is a reflection on brokenness. The boy Hugo seeks a message from his lost father through a clockwork robot that needs to be fixed. At first, he is troubled by its brokenness: 'A broken machine always makes me a little sad, because it isn't able to do what it was meant to do.' Towards the end of the film, Hugo is heartbroken when he accidentally breaks the now-repaired robot. He apologises to Georges, its original creator, saying, 'I'm sorry. It's broken.' Georges replies, 'No, it's not. It worked perfectly!' And so it did, because in this very brokenness, the object has brought together the stories of the two key protagonists so that both of their lives are transformed forever.

I wonder whether we dare make our own confession, 'I'm sorry. I'm broken,' to which God can reply, 'No, you are not. I can work perfectly in your weakness.'

Pause to reflect

- Make this your prayer:

  Almighty God,
  in Christ, you make all things new:
  transform the poverty of our nature by the riches of
      your grace,
  and in the renewal of our lives
  make known your heavenly glory;
  through Jesus Christ your Son our Lord.

REINTEGRATION

4

HOW ARE YOU BEING?

Emerging from my encounter with brokenness, I identified closely with clay-jar imagery. I had been smashed to pieces through overwork, stress, damaged health and lack of self-care. Now I was being patiently and gently glued back together. Once again, I could allow light to shine. However, the jar was now unstable. Sudden jolts caused me to wobble. Sustained pressure tested the glued joints and threatened to break me apart again. If this lamp was to continue to shine, I now needed not only not to be ill-treated but actually to be well-treated. It was surprising and disturbing what an alien concept this was for me.

I still longed sometimes to return to some previous strength and capability. I was frustrated by my sensitivity to disturbance and my ongoing fragility. However, increasingly, my challenge was to live with a chosen acceptance of my weaknesses as well as my strengths.

Serving God in vulnerability is, in the end, the only way, because it is true to our nature and experience as well as true to how God has made us and chosen to work through us. However, that does not mean that we are left exposed to the vagaries of circumstance or forced to live on the edge of coping, awaiting the next time we face the threat of disintegration. In fact, the discovery that we are fragile, together with the willingness to embrace that, makes it even more necessary that we know how to care for ourselves. We need to learn what it means to live an integrated life which sustains effective ministry in the long run.

Permission to self-care

This begins with the permission to self-care. Did you know it is all right to look after yourself as a Christian? That may sound obvious, but my conversations with many Christians suggest that we either do not know this or are not practising it.

We are deeply infected by the world's activist culture. It has not always been so. In 1992, Parker Palmer, speaking on 'Faith or frenzy', noted that in earlier centuries contemplation was the preferred life, followed by academia. An active life was perceived as one of tedious toil, where one did not have time to reflect on a higher plane. Over time that changed, and an active life became more prominent as technology progressed.[45]

We find ourselves trying harder, working longer, breathing heavier and getting wearier, so that we end up sour, stale, bored and numb. We may not admit it, but we become tired of God and of God's people. This falls far short of Jesus' invitation to fullness of life!

The possibility of self-care evokes all sorts of tensions within us. Many of us are unsure whether it is okay to look after ourselves. A faithful church volunteer commented, 'We're committed to being "sold-out" Christians but this ministry is damaging me and my family. Is it okay to pull back from caring for others when it becomes toxic to ourselves?' Torn between her commitment as a Christian and fulfilling responsibilities as a wife, mother and volunteer, let alone to herself, she was being pulled apart. The rhetoric of being a sacrificial Christian had left her unsure whether it was possible to be faithful to God and also to look after herself. She is by no means alone in this dilemma.

There are many places in scripture that feed this message. The language of taking up our cross daily, being a living sacrifice, leaving behind family and possessions, putting God and others first, is clear and true. For the faithful Christian, such language is a strong incentive to put self well down the pecking order. Add to that words of exhortation from the likes of Charles Spurgeon – 'Kill yourself with labour, and then pray yourself alive again'[46] – and the temptation to keep on keeping on whatever the cost is strong indeed. We end up like Bilbo Baggins: 'I feel thin, sort of stretched, like butter scraped over too much bread.'[47]

However, to be self-destructive is not the same as being self-sacrificial. Of course, there is a cost to discipleship, but that cost is not supposed to be working yourself into ill-health, marital breakdown and dried-out spirituality. The sacrifice Paul calls for is a living sacrifice – in stark contrast to the slaughtered sacrifices of his time. Our sacrificial lives need to be sustainable enough for us to go on giving. Remember, Jesus not only called us to take up our cross, but also invited us to come to him for rest, to find the 'unforced rhythms of grace' and the well-fitting yoke (Matthew 11:28–30, MSG).

Where and how do we find that balance?

Kate Rugani in the online magazine Faith & Leadership tells the story of Jeanette Hicks at a time when she had not yet found that balance. Six months into her ministry, this Methodist pastor admitted to being:

> a sleep-deprived wreck, surviving on sugar-fuelled energy and calorie-dense church meals. Despite... her best intentions, she was a walking portrait of exhaustion, with dull hair, brittle fingernails and dark circles under her eyes... 'If I took time to eat, that was time away from getting something done.'[48]

We'll return to Jeanette shortly.

In the same article, Rugani reports that research by Duke Divinity School reveals how 'clergy of all ages often find it difficult to take care of themselves... On the long list of items that must be done every day, they often put themselves last.' And this means that they regularly do not get far enough down the list to attend to their own needs.

> Many pastors misunderstand self-care to mean 'self-ish', said [research director] Rae Jean Proeschold-Bell... 'Clergy recognize the importance of caring for themselves, but doing so takes a back seat to fulfilling their vocational responsibilities... They feel they need permission to take time to attend to their health.'[49]

The question is, from whom will they find that permission?

The reality is that church leaders get little help from members who generally do not see or understand all that we do. Many expect church leaders to be available 24 hours a day, seven days a week. Each member has their individual job description for the leader, generating an impossible task. One church member exhorted me that I didn't have to say yes to everyone, then in the next breath asked why I hadn't turned up to their group activity recently.

Denominational structures are reluctant to encourage self-care, as they attempt to spread fewer ministers across a larger number of churches. I have come across very few examples of denominational leadership actively encouraging self-care among their ministers. And where leadership is predominantly male, meetings of local leaders often become places of competitive strength displays rather than of shared weakness and mutual support.

Most powerful of all is our own interior voice that demands everything and fears that to give time to self is to take it away from others. In the face of such expectations, it's easy for pastors to fall into the trap of feeling guilty when they take time to care for themselves. This is particularly strong when we are susceptible to people-pleasing, as many of us who find ourselves in the helping professions are.

In a rare but encouraging move, the United Methodist Church of North Carolina initiated a programme that encouraged leaders to give themselves permission to self-care. They emphasised stress management and healthy eating, underscored with scripturally based reasons for taking care of themselves. They found that this scriptural connection is essential for clergy, as it makes caring for themselves a part of their calling, not an additional task to complete.

Here is Jeanette Hicks again, two years down the line, saying, 'We're not honoring the vessel that God has given us to work with when we [run ourselves into the ground]... Honoring our bodies and our time, taking sabbath – these are as important as caring for others.'[50]

The crucial element in self-care, according to the evidence, is to be intentional about it. Duke Divinity School undertook research that found that clergy who were flourishing, with positive mental-health scores, were distinguishable from those who were languishing in one key respect: flourishers attended to their own well-being. In fact, 94% of clergy with flourishing mental health were intentional about spending time on personal care.[51]

Self-care strategies

Let's pause here for some self-care strategies, gleaned from the above research, my own life and elsewhere.

- Self-care happens when we remember it is God we serve rather than finding affirmation from the people we serve or our own internal drives. This takes self-knowledge and discernment, as well as courage to resist those who would like to control our ministry.
- Self-care happens when we are proactive in taking care of our physical and mental health, by prioritising behaviours such as eating well, visiting the doctor, keeping fit and making time for personal relationships and interests.

- Self-care happens when we are intentional about investing in spiritual care, finding a pattern of prayer and Bible reading that works for us, keeping a regular sabbath and developing relationships of accountability with a spiritual director, mentor or peer group.

- Self-care happens when we are intentional about setting boundaries around our work and personal lives, fixing time off and then, crucially, communicating that clearly to those who need to know.

- Self-care happens when we learn how to manage technology. This is more about how we switch devices off than switch them on. Set times when you do not pick up calls, or filter them through voicemail, sharing emergencies around a team where possible. Use different email accounts or even separate phones for 'church' and 'personal' contacts. Unplug for an hour and free yourself from the constant notifications.

- Self-care happens when we are intentional about investing in relationships with other leaders and colleagues for support and encouragement, as well as with family and friends for downtime and relaxation.

- Self-care happens when we intentionally treat ourselves in some small way to build ourselves up, interrupt our routines or introduce an element of joy:

  - Start a compliments file. Document positive feedback to read when surrounded by criticism or ingratitude.
  - Remove something from your to-do list that's been there for ages and you know you will never do.
  - Schedule a few five-minute periods of 'play' throughout your day. Stuart Brown says, 'The opposite of play is not work, it is depression. Respecting our biologically programmed need for play can bring back excitement and newness to our job.'[52]
  - Fix a small annoyance at home that's been nagging you and allow yourself to feel satisfied!
  - Choose to do one thing per day just because it makes you happy.

- Edit your social media feeds, and take out excessively negative people.
- Intersperse your day with short bursts of physical activity.
- Make one small change to your diet for the week.
- Be still. Sit somewhere green, and be quiet for a few minutes.
- Read or watch something that will bring a smile to your face.
- Power nap. Twenty minutes can reduce your sleep deprivation and leave you ready for action.
- Check in with your emotions. Sit quietly and name without judgement what you're feeling.
- Make a small connection. Have a few sentences of conversation with someone you encounter in your day.
- Spend an hour doing something that nourishes you – reading, your hobby, visiting a museum or gallery, etc.
- Plan an additional day off in the near future. Switch off your phone, tell people you will be away and then do something new.

As the Duke Divinity School research shows, those who follow ways of creating a set of priorities that make room for self flourish in ministry, and as such find their ministry flourishes! Proeschold-Bell says, 'If you're wondering whether these basic strategies make a difference, they do... Even though they sound like good common sense, they are hard to enact – but worth it. They are what differentiated flourishing pastors.'[53]

And when we flourish, we are more able to impact the world around us. Jesus asks the challenging question 'What good is salt if it loses its saltiness?' (see Matthew 5:13). A concern for our distinctive kingdom impact on the world around us can lead us down the road of hard work and away from self-care. But, in fact, self-destructive hard work is the way of the world rather than of the kingdom. What is more, there will come a point at which we have nothing more to offer. Then we really will have lost our saltiness in a more profound way. Self-care keeps us salty.

Finally, notice that Jesus' most basic command expects self-love alongside love of God: 'Love your neighbour as yourself' (Matthew 22:39). We know that love of neighbour includes both words and actions, and that it is hypocritical to say 'I love my neighbour' while simultaneously doing them harm or failing to do them good. Yet when it comes to loving ourselves, we find it possible to do that all the time. We proclaim that we are loved by God, but then push ourselves beyond the limits of human energy. We neglect our relationships with God and with those around us, even while encouraging others to make these a priority. We fail to attend to our own health or to engage in activities that bring us life, and then wonder why we are unwell or unfit.

And so, even in our attempt to be faithful, we become hypocrites and our message of love is compromised both in what we are able to offer and also by the witness we share. Those outside the church look at us and say, 'If they are going to love me like they love themselves then I'm not interested!' Instead, can we learn to risk loving ourselves as we would seek to love others? Then we will have something beautiful to share that people will see first in our own lives and relationships. Parker Palmer writes:

> Self-care is never a selfish act – it is simply good stewardship of the only gift I have, the gift I was put on earth to offer others. Anytime we can listen to our true self and give it the care it requires, we do it not only for ourselves, but for the many others whose lives we touch.[54]

Pause to reflect

- How do you respond to the Parker Palmer quote above?
- Where do you agree? Where do you resist?
- Are there steps towards self-care you have been neglecting?
- How might you show love for yourself by building these into your life?
- What impact might that have on those around you?

Stress at the top

Stress is a cultural phenomenon that affects everyone at different times and to varying degrees. While those who serve within the church are no worse off than those in non-church environments, there are particular stressors that church leaders will experience.

Internal stressors include:

- *Identity* – The leader's identity can become too closely associated with their role. Psychiatrist Robert McAllister says, 'The clergyman seems to me to be constantly involved in his environment in a way that does not characterise any other profession.'[55]
- *Success* – We are called to a task in which success is hard to define, let alone measure. This can persuade ministers to 'prove' themselves by working long hours so that evidence of success becomes the full diary, hours worked and missed days off.
- *Guilt* – This is not least because we are engaged in a task that is both of eternal urgency and never finished. Added to this is guilt when leaders feel anger, hatred, jealousy, envy, desire, sexual attraction, despair or even apathy during ministry.
- *Perfectionism* – In a 'be perfect as I am perfect' faith (see Matthew 5:48), we can face an idealism that makes anything less than perfection hard to accept, especially within ourselves.
- *Sexuality* – This becomes a stressor when leaders have to operate outside of their usual gender roles or are forced to cope within an institution dominated by the other gender. It affects those whose sexual orientation has to be lived out in a church still struggling to agree on what is permissible. Finally, there are issues around the appropriate handling of intimate pastoral relationships both with opposite and same-sex recipients of care.

External stressors include:

- *Expectations* – These arise mostly from the church wanting a particular sort of leader, but are augmented by the local community's sense of public ownership of the church. This is allied to the experience of being caught between intransigent congregations and hierarchical structures that are sometimes seen as demanding, unappreciative and out of touch.

- *Monetary factors* – Compared to many, clergy are not poor. However, compared to other similar professions, ministry in most denominations remains the one with the worst financial support.
- *Lack of clergy* – The huge reduction in the number of clergy in major denominations creates its own stressors, as churches are combined or people have to cover two 'half-time' jobs. At the same time, reduced membership creates increased financial pressure around fundraising.
- *Colleague dynamics* – Colleagues are potentially a source of great support, but can also be a source of stress where there is a lack of trust and the presence of competition and rivalries.
- *Living on the patch* – Conditions can often be extremely stressful for the last group of professionals to live in the community to which they minister.
- *Family* – This can become a source of stress for those who are married or have children. There is conflict between a demanding vocation and the desire to support the family, often lived out in the 'goldfish bowl' of the vicarage.
- *Singleness* – Living alone creates a different set of issues around giving ourselves permission to take time out, as well as the potential for facing isolation and loneliness.

We can add to these a host of other stressors, such as the increasingly consumerist society that fosters demand for individual satisfaction from everything, including church. Local factors, such as urban deprivation or rural isolation, bring their own challenges. Finally, the nature of pastoral ministry confronts us with the best and worst of human behaviour. One senior cleric spoke of feeling sometimes as if he is confronted with a bottomless pit of dependency.

Stress is, of course, not necessarily a negative force. Positively, stress takes us beyond the bland, stimulates our cognitive and creative abilities, and creates within us the challenge to fight those stressors that invade our world, or, where appropriate, to flee from them.

However, stress can be destructive too. There are medical links between stress and coronary heart disease, cancer and asthma, along with the increased risk of infection. It can cause the sort of mental pressure that leads to breakdown, depression and burnout. It can drive people to do the sorts of things that damage personal and family life, as well as their ministry.

So what makes the difference? A useful distinction is that between stress, excess stress and distress. Stress is neutral. The problem comes when there is excess stress. The inability of the person to handle this and return to their comfort zone leads to distress. This may occur due to the breakdown in resistance that occurs in a period of continual bombardment; the lack of development of coping mechanisms; or when stress taps into existing unresolved personal trauma. However, the principal difference among those who find a way of coping with stress before it becomes distress is that they have developed a structure of personal care for themselves rather than remaining alone in their stress.

At the heart of personal care, some sort of relationship network within which stress can be identified and managed is vital. Unfortunately, this is precisely what many leaders lack. Opportunities for meaningful relationships are rare, and we find ourselves facing isolation or even choosing insulation. Thus, a vicious circle develops. Stress is isolating because it separates us from our existing relationships and may even damage them. At the same time, those very relationships hold within them the means of managing the stress we face.

In some traditions, a theology of priesthood that emphasises the separation of the priest contributes to this sense of being alone. Allied to this are historic models of training that accentuated a 'solo' rather than a corporate approach. Sometimes this was cashed out in a specific instruction to avoid friendships within the parish and to break contact when moving to a new parish. Although this is definitely changing, and there is now much talk of collaborative ministry, the reality on the ground appears to be that this solo approach is still surprisingly prevalent.

Pause to reflect

- Which of these stressors do you recognise in your own ministry?
- Did you realise that they were part of your experience?
- Where would you place yourself on a scale that goes from feeling stress through excess stress to distress?

Who am I?

If we are going to sustain leadership marked by vulnerability, while also facing the demands of the role, we need a good grasp of our identity. This, however, does not come automatically. John Ortberg asked his spiritual director, Dallas Willard, 'Why is it that I have a PhD in clinical psychology and a master of divinity and work as a pastor and yet I'm not sure who I am?' Willard answered him, 'The most important thing in your life is not what you do but who you become. That's what you will take into eternity.'[56]

In seeking firstly to know who we are, and then to be who we are, we are up against the fastest-changing, most connected world that has ever existed – a world that tends to keep us on the surface of things. Look around you on the train, in a coffee shop or walking down the street and you will see people so busy tuning into the world that they often haven't discovered how to tune into themselves.

Richard Rohr says:

> Most of us have lived our whole lives with a steady stream of... ideas, images, and feelings. We have to discover who this 'I'

really is, the one who has these always passing feelings and thoughts. Who am I behind my thoughts and feelings?[57]

James Joyce puts it simply and powerfully when he observes of one of his characters, 'Mr Duffy lived at a little distance from his body.'[58]

We will need to learn something about looking beneath the surface if we are to live slightly less distantly from ourselves and draw near to God. Some 1,600 years ago, Augustine of Hippo reflected, 'Men go abroad to wonder at the heights of mountains, the huge waves of the sea, the long courses of the rivers, the vast compass of the ocean, the circular motions of the stars, yet they pass by themselves without wondering.'[59]

Sometimes we use valuable energy manufacturing an identity that isn't ours. The eponymous character in *Veronika Decides to Die* by Paulo Coelho is described like this:

> She gave all her friends the impression that she was a woman to be envied, and she expended most of her energy in trying to behave in accordance with the image she had created of herself. Because of that she never had enough energy to be herself...[60]

Media commentator Revd Richenda Leigh reflected with me on the way so many are caught up with the cult of celebrity: 'Young people are hurting because they expect to feel on the inside how their celebrities look on the outside.'[61]

When I was a curate (a trainee vicar), I followed five highly gifted curates, and I desperately wanted to be the model curate. Then I looked up the word 'model' in the dictionary and found the definition: 'A small imitation of the real thing.' That should have prompted me to try to discover who I really was. But I am a slow learner, so it was only much more recently and through many trials that I was able to write this in my journal:

> I have learned that the person I am is not the person I thought I was. This is good news, because the person I thought I was is the person I thought I needed to be – and I could never quite be that person. Now I am free to be the person I truly am!

One of the greatest enemies of the ability to be ourselves comes from the threat of making comparisons. Brené Brown speaks of how 'the comparison mandate becomes this crushing paradox of "fit in and stand out! Be just like everyone else, but better."'[62] How draining it is to spend such enormous amounts of energy conforming and competing.

Help, I'm an addict

We are all needy people! The first of the twelve steps of Alcoholics Anonymous is an acknowledgement of need. To a greater or lesser extent, we all live with a host of insecurities that, whether or not we realise it, impact on the things we do and say. Few of us are truly free from the need to make other people think we are good or likeable. These are things we do because we are addicts. We like to be liked. We desire affirmation. We need to be noticed. We yearn for self-worth. We want to be useful. Some may thirst for power or crave being in control. Becoming the leader of a church or ministry will not automatically preserve you from this; in fact, it may offer the perfect arena to those unacknowledged needs!

Henri Nouwen confesses:

> Against my own best intentions I find... [w]hen I give advice, I want to know whether it is being followed; when I offer help, I want to be thanked; when I give money, I want it to be used my way; when I do something good, I want to be remembered.[63]

Awareness of our desire to be valued is important whatever form our ministry might take. There is a danger that our neediness may cause us, in the very act of laying down our lives, to build up our own ego instead. But when we serve from our ego we are not giving freely, the way Jesus does.

The beautiful shepherd

Jesus calls himself the good shepherd. Actually, 'good' is better translated as 'beautiful' – not in the sense of physical beauty, but more like attractive or inspiring. Jesus is the beautiful shepherd who draws people to himself. This beauty is not a level of moral goodness that we have to attain; rather, 'The [beautiful] shepherd lays down his life for the sheep' (John 10:11).

We read this and jump straight to the cross as the supreme example, but this beauty is not specifically referring to a way of dying so much as to a way of living – a way of living each moment of every day, whatever the cost may be.

And the really important aspect of the way Jesus lays down his life is that it is a free choice, through which he reveals his Father's love. 'No one takes [my life] from me, but I lay it down of my own accord' (John 10:18). Like us, Jesus faces a moment-by-moment decision to either build up his ego or to lay down his life. The beauty we see in Jesus is that he consistently and freely chooses to lay down his life. And the outcome is that Jesus lives a life immersed in his Father's love: 'The reason my Father loves me is that I lay down my life' (John 10:17). This cannot mean that he earns the Father's love. It's more that Jesus' way of living both reveals and releases the Father's love. Stephen Verney translates the phrase as: 'Through this the Father's love actually comes alive in me.'[64]

If we could really gaze on this beauty of Jesus, then we would be transformed, as would the world around us, because to see the beauty might lead us nearer to being the beauty too.

The response to this is not to crank up the effort of our servanthood. Rather, we should identify whether, like Jesus, our life is laid down freely, because it is easy to lay down our life either for the wrong reasons or at the very least with mixed motives.

We don't intend to do that, and we might not even realise that's what we're doing. Our hearts are good at covering up what is really going on. We may not be able to see what we are doing until some hardship arrives to undermine and unveil the ego. But, for those with ears to hear, there are some clues.

A good way to test how much we need, rather than choose, to serve is to ask, 'Is what I give given freely if I cannot also choose not to give? Am I freely offering myself or am I being compelled by some inner drive?' It was only when I was forced through ill health to stop serving that I discovered how much I needed to be needed. It's not what I thought I had been doing or what I had intended to do, but part of me had been meeting my own neediness even as I gave myself to others. I spoke to a retired priest who had completely finished all active ministry. 'How are you coping with that?' I asked. 'Not very well,' he admitted. He felt less of a person.

The question of our identity – 'Who am I?' – is often confused with the question of our role – 'What do you do?' A father asks his little girl, 'What do you want to be when you grow up?' to which she replies, 'I want to be happy!' 'No,' insists the father, 'what do you want to do?' Still the standard opening question when meeting people for the first time is 'What do you do?' How do we introduce ourselves?

When I was a marketing manager I had a straightforward response to that standard question. Later, I could introduce myself as a mature student training for ordination, before taking on admittedly confusing titles like curate, vicar and associate minister. But what now? I am an 'early-retired priest' (I still emphasise the 'early' part of this!). But that doesn't define what I do. For three years I could offer the holy-sounding title 'Bishop's Adviser on Spirituality', but now

I am attempting to inhabit a countercultural world in which I do not need a title to define who I am. Sometimes that seems like a really terrible idea. It is certainly challenging!

You are more important than your ministry!

Within this existential identity confusion, here is some good news to ground us and to bring the deepest encouragement: God is much more interested in who we are than what we do. In fact, I would say:

You are more important than your ministry!

In a way, this is what this book is about. *You are more important than your ministry!*

Whether that feels like good news or not might be revealing. We may be uncomfortable with this revolutionary idea. Surely our ministry is what really matters to God. But this phrase is a vital counter to our tendency to define ourselves by our work. We need to hear this repeated often and also to live it day by day. The paradox is that the busier you are the more loudly you need to hear it said, because the harder it will be to hear.

I first heard this truth when my busy ministry came to a sudden end. A frequent response to that happening was 'It seems such a waste of your ministry for it to end in this way.' Of course, people meant well in trying to affirm my ministry and acknowledge their sadness that I couldn't continue, but I didn't find it helpful, largely because it was something I was thinking myself, unacknowledged and hidden under the surface of my new existence.

As I battled this internal dialogue, I took it to God in prayer. Immediately, though not audibly, I heard very clearly from God: 'You are more important than your ministry.'

I was overwhelmed with the surprising discovery that I mattered to God independent of what I was doing for him. I had long trusted that I was loved, but part of my journey of faith had always made a strong connection between belonging to God and serving him. And somehow, over years of service, my sense of value as a person had fallen behind the value I placed on what I was doing for God. I now realise that this false understanding gave me permission to consistently prioritise ministry over self-care.

While I don't believe that God sent disaster to teach me this lesson, he did use the traumatic circumstances to help me begin to get things the right way round. There were issues I needed to attend to, be healed of and grow in that could not be fitted in while I was also running a church. To my enormous surprise, instead of God saying that my stuff could wait because my ministry was so important, he said, 'You have got to come first!'

To believe my ministry was the important thing pandered to my ego, but damaged my soul. To discover that I was more important than my ministry was unwelcome to my ego, but real nourishment to my soul. My ego had to take the necessary hit in acknowledging that I was not indispensable. And, with characteristically sharp humour, God pressed the point home: the person he called to take over my leadership of the church was plucked from literally the far side of the world to grow and develop the work.

The tremendously affirming discovery that I mattered should not have been a surprise. Scripture is clear that God has always been able to manage without 'key people' being in front-line ministry for a while. Moses spent years in the wilderness. David was anointed as king, then immediately returned to shepherding. Jesus lived in obscurity for 30 of his 33 years. After Paul's dramatic conversion, he spent three years in the desert. The desert, the place of apparent barrenness, is often the place God takes us to in order to do his deep work. And while we are there, the world continues to turn and the seeds of the kingdom continue to grow.

We all need regular reminders that we are not defined by our level of busyness. That's not always what we hear from the church. Leadership meetings are interrupted by the steady vibration of multiple smartphones declaring how busy we are. Many are proud of not taking days off, or of how long people will have to wait before we can squeeze a meeting into their busy diaries, as if it would be embarrassing to say, 'I'm available this week.' One of the values I now embrace is to leave spaces in my diary, as a means of offering the rare gift of availability to others and as a caution not to justify myself with the fullness of my calendar.

The primacy of being

We need to be reminded regularly that busyness was never God's intention for us. In the beginning, Adam and Eve had the calling of caring for creation, but that task flowed out of their relationship with God. In the evening of each day (the start of the Hebrew day) they would walk in the garden with God and enjoy being together.

Perhaps the simplest way of summarising the Old Testament covenant is in these oft-repeated words: 'I will *be* your God and you will *be* my people' (see, for example, Exodus 6:7; Jeremiah 7:23; 11:4; 30:22; Ezekiel 36:28).

It is not surprising, therefore, that when Jesus calls the disciples, Mark tells us that he calls them first to be *with* him and only then to go and do ministry *for* him. In John's gospel, when Jesus encounters John's disciples, he asks them, 'What are you looking for?' They answer, 'Rabbi… where are you staying?' (John 1:38, NRSV). This strange response conveys a desire to be where Jesus is and then to stay there – to abide.

At the end of Jesus' earthly ministry, he tells his disciples not to begin their mission to the world until he has come to dwell within them in the person of the Spirit (Acts 1:4–5).

You can see why I have entitled this chapter 'How are you being?' We don't usually get asked that question. We are more familiar with 'How are you doing?' But it is a good question to ask in order to keep in touch with the question 'Who am I?'

Training consultant Liz Guthridge advises people to stay in touch with who they are by asking at least once a day, 'How am I being?' To make this even more practical, she suggests creating a 'to-be list' alongside our to-do list to help us become more aware, focused and healthy so that we can perform at our peak. Her example to-be list includes:

- Be present.
- Be calm.
- Be curious.
- Be kind.
- Be observant.
- Be tolerant.
- Be relaxed.[65]

Other responses I have heard are:

- Be patient.
- Be prayerful.
- Be joyful.
- Be trusting.
- And my favourite unexpected response, from someone seeking to respond more spontaneously to God rather than constantly ticking the boxes of an oppressive to-do list: be inefficient.

Guthridge says:

> When you start being more mindful about how you want to be and act, you start adopting this state of mind and set of behaviours... Living and working with intention helps us break the cycle of craving to be busy for the sake of being busy.[66]

Brené Brown's research on wholeheartedness also revealed some informative lists.[67] The to-be lists of wholehearted people were brimming with words like worthy, resting, playful, trusting, faithful, intuitive, hopeful, authentic, loving, joyful, grateful and creative. The contrasting 'don't-be' column contained words like perfect, numbing, certain, exhausted, self-sufficient, cool, fitting in and judging. Those who managed to live more in their 'be' column than their 'don't-be' column were more likely to live wholehearted lives.

Of course, this apparently contemporary tool is not really new. The Bible has two challenging to-be lists. In the sermon on the mount, Jesus provides a to-be list that is both a descriptor of himself and an invitation to ways in which we can grow into his likeness. This countercultural list of be-attitudes includes being poor in spirit, willing to mourn, humble, hungry for righteousness, merciful, pure, a peacemaker and even persecuted. Challenging though these ways of being are, Jesus declares them to be blessed places of receiving the kingdom, being comforted, inheriting the earth, being filled, receiving mercy, seeing God and being called God's children (Matthew 5:3–12).

We know Paul's to-be list from Galatians as the fruit of the Spirit, produced in those who walk in step with the Spirit. This fruit is comprised of 'love, joy, peace, forbearance, kindness, goodness, faithfulness, gentleness and self-control' (Galatians 5:22–23).

When I read these Bible to-be lists, my response is 'Yes, that's what I want to be when I grow up!'

Pause to reflect

Spend some time compiling a to-be list. You may find it helpful to reflect first on either Matthew 5:3–12 or Galatians 5:22–23.

Looking beneath the surface

After conducting an in-depth study of 72 high-performing CEOs, Cornell University researchers reached a surprising conclusion. The key predictor of success for leaders wasn't focus, education, decision-making, strategic planning or even IQ. It was self-awareness.[68]

Christian singer and broadcaster Sheila Walsh shares this testimony:

> One morning I was sitting on national television with my nice suit and that night I was in the locked ward of a psychiatric hospital. The psychiatrist asked me, 'Who are you?' 'I'm the co-host of a TV show.' 'That's not what I meant,' he said. 'I'm a writer and a singer.' 'That's still not what I meant. Who are you?' 'I don't have a clue,' I said. And he replied, 'That's why you are here.'[69]

Sheila's experience reinforces the cruciality of self-awareness concerning Identity. This is particularly important for those who serve, because if our service does not come from a healthy sense of who we are, we may end up serving ourselves and our needs to the detriment of others and, paradoxically, to our own detriment too.

The first step is very simple: ask the question 'Who am I?' We make our own choice to search much deeper within. Often the question is forced upon us by crisis. For many, this is uncharted territory. We've become so used to living on the surface of our lives that we've forgotten there's anything else.

Iceberg ahead?

Peter Scazzero's image of 'iceberg spirituality' is challenging.[70] Ninety per cent of an iceberg lies beneath the water's surface, and that is the part most likely to cause a shipwreck. Many times, we see relationships, churches and ministries sabotaged by people responding out of the issues that lie unacknowledged beneath the surface.

A long-standing church member was asked to move seats for a service led by the bishop in case the bishop's wife needed a seat near the front. In the end, the bishop's wife sat somewhere else and the seat remained unused. That long-standing member never returned to church.

A normally gentle man stood in front of me following a Remembrance service and shouted in my face, because we had marginally mistimed the 11.00 am silence. He later phoned to apologise, saying that his watch was fast!

Two talented assistant leaders in a parachurch organisation were up for promotion. When one was appointed, the other resigned and withdrew from an area of ministry for which he was supremely gifted.

We could all recount many such stories. Here's how one person put it: 'I was a Christian for 22 years. But instead of being a 22-year-old Christian, I was a one-year-old Christian 22 times!'[71]

The starting point for any journey of growth is admitting that something is wrong. I have been a Christian now for the same time God's people spent wandering in the wilderness. I wonder how many times I've gone around in circles as far as maturity is concerned? I have discovered that getting older does not automatically make me more mature. I look at my ageing face in the mirror and wonder how I can often still feel as weak, moody and vulnerable as ever!

How are we doing in the church with loving one another as Christ has loved us? What about the instruction not to complain? To give generously? To forgive as we are forgiven? It's not that we don't know these things, but my observation is that we have some way to go. Often our destructive surface behaviour is a consequence of unacknowledged 'iceberg stuff' under the surface.

The pressures of grinding to a halt in ministry and the wide-open desert of the aftermath gave me plenty of time to reflect on this. And time is needed, because we are not good at looking under the surface of our lives. Most of us will, if we're honest, admit that there are deep layers beneath our day-to-day awareness. There are visible changes that others can see on the surface of our lives, but large chunks remain hidden and untouched, and these may be the real reason for how we respond to challenges. Dare we ask ourselves 'Am I any different on the inside than the outside? Are my inner thought life and my outer visible life integrated, or am I in danger of disintegrating as I try to hold them together?'

This is not simply about avoiding disaster. We go under the surface so that we can know God. Augustine of Hippo asked, 'How can you draw close to God when you are far from your own self?' And he prayed, 'Grant, Lord, that I may know myself that I may know you.'[72]

When we dare to pray that prayer, two things become clear. First, we begin to notice the disguises we often use, both when projecting ourselves to the world and to protect ourselves from the world.

Second, we notice that to be in the image of God means we have emotions. Psychologists identify a vast range of emotions, but these are the ones that recur time and time again: anger, sadness, love, joy, shame, disgust, surprise and fear. The problem is we don't always know the full range of our feelings because we have learned to ignore or bury those we find uncomfortable. But to bury emotions is always to bury them alive! For a long time, I lived within a narrow band of emotions – with no great highs or great lows. I have since learned that this was part of a long-established defence system which successfully kept all emotions under check.

Dan Allender and Tremper Longman warn that 'Ignoring our emotions is turning our back on reality; listening to our emotions ushers in reality. And reality is where we meet with God.'[73] In neglecting our intense emotions, we therefore not only become false to ourselves but also lose a wonderful opportunity to know God. We forget that change comes through brutal honesty and vulnerability before God. It's no good simply to attend another conference, read another book or go for prayer one more time if we are not dealing with the underlying issues.

And this is a battleground. As we address the 'Who am I?' question we need to be wary of the traps of the enemy.[74] In his wilderness testing (Matthew 4:1–11), the key question for Jesus was one of identity: 'If you are who you say you are, then...' This testing was vital to Jesus in clarifying his purpose. We too can learn to resist the temptation to find identity in the wrong places.

Identity as performance: I am what I do

'If you are the Son of God, tell these stones to become bread' (Matthew 4:3). At a time when Jesus was alone and hungry, had 'done nothing' and had recruited no followers, the temptation was to do something to define his identity. He was able to do it; later, he turned bread into more bread. But this was a question of identity and he knew he was more than what he did.

Our culture asks the same: 'What have you achieved? Are you any use? What do you do?' But is that who we really are? What if we lose our job or can't find one? What if our area of work is one which is not that impressive to others.

When identity is defined by performance, we can be driven beyond our capacity or left feeling worthless. We eventually find, as Thomas

Merton noted, that we spent the whole of our lives climbing the ladder only to reach the top and find that it was leaning against the wrong wall![75]

Identity as possessions: I am what I have

Jesus was offered all the magnificence of the earth in contrast to the nothing he possessed at that time. There is great irony in offering the one through whom all things were made a slice of his own creation, but Jesus knew that he could not be defined by what he had.

Our culture assigns great value to what we own, believing that without anything you're a nobody. The marketing industry spends billions persuading us to measure ourselves by who has the most, the biggest, the latest. Status at work is based around perks and titles. In the company for which I worked people competed with one another for pay rises, company cars, the floor area of their office space and even the comfort of their office chair. It's very hard for us to truly discover who we are while we fall prey to the temptation that the root of security lies in what we possess. Stephen Levine says:

> If you made a list of everything you own, everything you think of as you… that list would be the distance between you and the living truth. In contrast, there is freedom for the one who can say: 'The Lord is my Shepherd, therefore I lack nothing' (Psalm 23:1).[76]

Identity as popularity: I am what others think

Jesus' third temptation was to make a big impression by jumping off the temple. At the start of his public ministry, what a temptation it was for Jesus to get things started with a spectacular stunt. But Jesus knows not to find his identity in popularity. Later, he challenges people about the cost of following him. Another time, as people walk away from him in droves, Jesus is secure enough to risk asking his friends if they also want to leave.

Our culture places such a high premium on what other people think that we can become popularity addicts. We must learn to spot when we find that the slightest praise causes us to soar and mild criticism to sink. Sheila Walsh agrees:

> I measured myself by what other people thought of me and it was slowly killing me.[77]

Peering under the surface

Teresa of Avila said, 'Almost all problems in the spiritual life stem from a lack of self-knowledge.'[78] Dare we look under the surface to what lies beneath? Here are some steps towards greater self-awareness that may help you to avoid shipwrecks.

Listen to your body

We may have become unintentionally good at self-deception, but our bodies never lie. We can develop awareness of what we are feeling by paying attention to our body: a knot in the stomach, a tension headache, teeth-grinding, hand-wringing and insomnia are all powerful clues that something is amiss. We can then ask, 'What might my body be telling me?' In the end, my body became so frustrated by my refusal to listen that it just shut down altogether.

Pay attention to your inner thoughts in the place of silence

The place of silence is where all those thoughts going on under the surface are allowed to have their voice. The struggle is not about preventing such thoughts from arising – repression and suppression will not help. It is about returning again and again to focus on God in us so that we become grounded in his love. As we notice the persistent thoughts that rise up from within, we observe them passing by but not so much that we lose our intimate connection with God. Like Elijah getting past the earthquake, wind and fire before he could hear God's gentle whisper (1 Kings 19:9–18), we can come back to our thoughts later through prayers for help or healing, or through confession of sin, noting the need to have a conversation or complete a task or to simply let something go.

Imagine a large water tank filled with ping-pong balls. The balls represent your underlying feelings. Often, life is an attempt to keep all those balls under the surface. If one escapes our grasp and pops to the surface, we grab it instinctively and plunge it back under before we or others notice. We do so using strategies such as busyness, distraction, addictions, surface living and so on. To risk sitting on our own, in solitude and silence, is to stop playing that game for a while. It is risky, but it allows the hidden to rise to the surface. There, some concerns will float away because they are not as significant as we feared. Others will remain and provide us with an agenda for prayer, healing or support.

One of the early church fathers, Abba Moses, said, 'Go, sit in your cell, and your cell will teach you everything.'[79]

Ask searching questions

Ian Cron recommends pausing to ask three questions to improve self-awareness in the face of life's tests. First, 'What am I believing right now?' The answer to that question can be quite surprising. Second, 'Are these beliefs true?' Often we find we are believing something quite untrue, like 'I need to be a success in this.' Finally, we are free to ask, 'How would my life change if I let go of this belief?'[80]

Find trusted companions

This journey begins in solitude, but usually it cannot be completed alone. We need trusted companions to help us along the way. Our own ability to self-deceive is much more insidious than we think. That's why we need to seek out those who will walk with us and, where necessary, confront us. They may include mentors, spiritual directors, counsellors, mature friends, members of a small group or leadership team, or peer support groups. Sometimes those closest to us know us better than we know ourselves.

If you don't have a trusted companion, then ask God and let him surprise you! Tessi Rickabaugh writes:

> I'm not telling lies on purpose… Whatever my reason, it's the quiet, steady gaze of my spiritual director that guides me past my self-deception and invites me to join her on a quest for my deepest truth. It is a quest well worth the effort.[81]

Use carefully researched tools to understand your personality

Every tool is, in the end, just that, but they provide insights into who we are, how we function, from where we find our energy and what our potential weaknesses and strengths are. They are another resource that takes us beyond our subjective concept of who we are and how we function into something more objective. Two tools I have found particularly helpful are the Myers-Briggs Type Indicator and the Enneagram.[82]

Move out of your comfort zone

Dying to our false self and allowing our true self to emerge is frightening. Anything that takes us beyond our known circle of comfort brings fear and stress. The temptation is to withdraw into what we know. But the reward for pushing on through will be to enlarge our circle of comfort. We will learn new skills, feel new emotions, try new ways of being and praying. We can discover that it is all right to receive a compliment; that to say no will not bring an end to life as we know it; that to admit weakness does not make the roof fall in; or that to engage with conflict does not lead to death of friendship.

The greatest gift we can give the world is that of our true self living in the love of God. I love the tale of Rabbi Zusya, who said, 'In the coming world, they will not ask me, why were you not Moses? They will ask me, why were you not Zusya?'[83]

Pause to reflect

- Draw an iceberg, with 90% of it below the water line. In the top ten per cent write words describing how you show yourself to others. On the lower 90% note thoughts, behaviours and feelings that remain hidden below the surface. Which 'you' does God see?
- As you journey beneath the surface find trusted companions to walk with you.

Recovering our core identity

These warnings about locating our identity in the wrong places, together with the encouragement to self-awareness, lead us to return to the subject of recovering core identity.

Richard Rohr tells the parable of a young child who, when his brother is born, asks if he can speak to the baby alone. Fascinated, the parents listen at the door to discover what he wants to ask the newborn baby. This is what they hear: 'Quick, tell me where you came from. I am beginning to forget already!'[84] We so easily forget who we are. Perhaps Jesus has this in mind when he urges us to become like little children to 'get' the kingdom. We need frequent reminders of who we objectively are.

Archbishop Justin Welby faced this identity challenge himself. When he found out in 2016 that his father was not who he had thought, it generated a media storm. The news would have been devastating to many people, but Welby took it in his stride because he knew, deep down, this truth: 'I know that I find who I am in Jesus Christ, not in genetics, and my identity in him never changes.'[85] This reveals his strong grasp on his true rather than his false self. Your true self is the part of you that knows who you are and whose you are. Your false self is just who you think you are, or even who you think you need to be.

One of the most powerful identity-defining statements of Jesus is this: 'Do not rejoice that the spirits submit to you, but rejoice that your names are written in heaven' (Luke 10:20). If we could fully trust this, it would change our whole life agenda and root us in the deep knowledge of our true self. Our identity is not in the success of the latest task but in our belonging to God. This knowledge does not lead to pride, but instead makes all posturing and pretending unnecessary. Richard Rohr concludes, 'Our core anxiety that we are not good enough is resolved from the beginning, and we can stop all our climbing, contending, criticising and competing. All "accessorising" of any small fragile self henceforth shows itself to be a massive waste of time.'[86]

When we are able to move beyond our false self, it does not feel like a loss; rather that we have gained a new freedom to be who we were always intended to be. An unattributed quote says, 'Be yourself: everyone else is already taken.'[87]

We know this, but, as in the story of the little boy and his baby brother, we forget. And the more we find ourselves doing things for God the more quickly we return to finding our identity in what we do rather than who we are. Looking back on my story, there was more of that going on for me than I realised. Now I am finally reaching a place where I can say that it is good for me that I can no longer do for God what I once was able to do. In my weakness, I am forced to rely on grace more than anything else – including works! It's still hard though. I still regularly want to go back to the old 'normal'.

Henri Nouwen invites us to define ourselves as radically loved by God.[88] Many times, I have allowed the distraction of work or the assault of trials to lead me away, like a prodigal, from this place of security to a far-off land of isolation and scarcity. One day, as I was struggling with low self-esteem and the battle to recover from the bleakest parts of my journey, I complained to God, 'This is too hard for me to do!' Swiftly and firmly, but with extreme gentleness, came the response: 'Is it too hard to be my son?'

Sometimes it takes a fall to discover what it means to be loved by God in our poverty. Then we fall into the relief of that knowledge even as we are embarrassed and surprised by the scandal of this thing called grace. Niels Bohr said, 'If you are not profoundly shocked by quantum physics you have not understood it!'[89] With apologies, I would say the same about grace. A man admitted to me his struggle to believe that God could love him in the face of his many failures. I responded, 'Grace would be easier to accept if we felt we deserved it in some way. But then it wouldn't be grace.' Jody Cross writes:

> Through many painful lessons... I have realised that I can't make anything happen. I am not large and in charge. I am not the great one. Actually... I am small and weak. Journeying... with my faithful, sanctifying, ever-patient Lord, I am learning that the poor in spirit are blessed. I am learning that His power is made perfect in my weakness, and I am learning how great and amazing are His deeds.[90]

It is just as Jesus, the apostle Paul, Francis of Assisi, John of the Cross, Thérèse of Lisieux, Brennan Manning, Mother Teresa, Sheila Cassidy, Henri Nouwen, Jean Vanier and many more witnesses teach us: there is incredible power in powerlessness! Belonging in the kingdom comes through a willingness to discover our ultimate value even as we face up to the reality of our smallness and incapacity. Our conscious need for mercy is our only real boarding pass. The ego does not like that very much, but the soul understands.

Like the prodigal son, we usually need a crisis so that we come to our senses and say, 'My way isn't working. Maybe there is another way of being.' The good news is that we do not need to earn God's love because he has already given it to us in Jesus. Through our incorporation in him we too can hear the Father's baptismal affirmation: 'You are my Son, whom I love; with you I am well pleased' (see Mark 1:11).

Here, in these words spoken from heaven to Jesus before he began his public ministry, we do indeed have everything we need. This is our core identity: to fully belong as children of God.

We have the most profound and unchanging *belonging* as we hear our maker say, 'You are my child.' Belonging is such an innate human desire that we try to acquire it by fitting in or seeking approval. These are not only hollow substitutes for belonging, but often barriers to it. Brené Brown differentiates between belonging and fitting in. Fitting in, she says, is about assessing a situation and becoming who you need to be in order to be accepted. Belonging, on the other hand, doesn't require us to change who we are; it gives us permission to be who we are.[91] To hear for ourselves the voice that says, 'You are my child,' is true belonging.

Added to belonging is the gift of *being loved*. The God who calls us his child also says, 'I love you.' Love and belonging are held together. A deep knowledge of love and belonging is an irreducible need of all women, men and children. We are biologically, cognitively, physically and spiritually wired to love and to be loved. When those needs are not met, we don't function as we were meant to. We fall apart. We hurt, and we hurt others. We get sick. However, to truly hear the voice that says, 'I love you,' is healing indeed.

Finally, belonging and being loved have added to them *affirmation*: 'You are my child, whom I love; *with you I am well pleased*.' This echoes the 'very good' acclamation by God at creation, when humanity had not yet achieved anything (Genesis 1:31). At his baptism, although Jesus had yet to begin his ministry, his Father was well pleased with him. God has chosen to invite us into that relationship of unconditional pleasure and affirmation. This is an 'I love you' with no ifs, buts or whens. This is an 'I love you' with an immediate full stop, which, paradoxically, infers it will go on forever, uninterrupted by anything we will ever think or say or do.

To hear that we belong, are loved and are approved of is a powerful combination that alone can set us free from needing to find belonging in any other way, to seek love in any of its substitutes or to win the approval of anyone else. However, it will take some time to realise this truth, to live in it and to extricate ourselves from the tentacles of a lifetime of finding our identity elsewhere.

Julian of Norwich had an extraordinary revelation of the love of God. The promise she received was:

> The place which God takes in our soul he will never vacate, for in us is his home of homes, and it is the greatest delight for him to dwell there… The soul who contemplates this is made like the one who is contemplated.[92]

So a good question to ask is, 'Where is the place and what are the times when you dwell in the knowledge of God's love for you just as you are?' It will be out of those experiences that we can more freely serve others.

As I travelled to address a group I feared would be critical, I noticed anxiety levels rising and my heart beating ever faster. Checking out what was happening under the surface, I found, to my discomfort, that even though I was nominally serving others, I was actually in need of affirmation from the group. Once I realised that, I was able to remind myself that I had all I needed through my core identity. I repeated out loud, 'I do not need anything from these people!' Now I was more free to go and serve, to offer what I felt God wanted me to share rather than subtly trying to work out how to get what I needed from them.

Of course, this is not a one-off lesson. As a 'please-aholic', I need to repeat it with each encounter, letting go of getting what I think I need; taking hold of what I have from God; and then finding that I am even able to lay down my life a little – freely, as a choice – like Jesus shows us.

At first, that might look very similar to the sort of servanthood that arises from mixed motives. God's grace is such that he uses even our distorted motives to minister to others, because it really is all about him. It may even have the same impact. But inside there is a world of difference. Serving freely will be life-giving rather than life-sapping. Free from needing it to be all about you, you can begin to find, as Jesus did, what it means for the Father's love to come alive in you.

Henri Nouwen asks:

> Can I give without wanting anything in return, love without attaching any conditions? Considering my immense need for human recognition, I realise it will be a lifelong struggle. But I am also convinced that each time I step over this need and act free of my concern for return, I can trust that my life can truly bear the fruits of God's Spirit.[93]

At the end of the film *Starter for 10* (dir. Tom Vaughan, 2006), the lead character, Brian Jackson, played by James McAvoy, asks his girlfriend whether she can ever forgive all his stupidity. Her response to this person who has prided himself throughout on his ability to answer the hardest University Challenge questions is simply this: 'You already know the answer to that question!'

Fifteenth-century mystic Margery Kempe, an extraordinary character who was the first woman to write an autobiography in English, was anxious for years about whether she had done enough to merit God's favour. Once, as she prayed, she heard God say to her: 'More pleasing to me than all your prayers, works and penances is that you would believe that I love you.'[94]

Pause to reflect

- Sit comfortably somewhere quiet, hold out your hands and look down at them.
- Consciously let go of all the worthy things you could bring to God as the work of your hands. Instead, focus on your empty, wounded and scarred hands.
- Experience the grace of staying in that place empty-handed before the God who loves you, is pleased with you and calls you his beloved child.

5

RESTORING OUR IMAGE OF GOD

What sort of God do we serve?

I wanted to dramatise the Bible reading at an all-age service, so I invited someone to be the 'voice of God', hidden in the vestry with a microphone. As he delivered his lines, I immediately noticed that the voice my volunteer used for God was far removed from his own normal voice. It sounded harsh, authoritarian, angry and distant – none of which matched the mood of the story. Later, I thanked him and asked whether he had noticed the tone of voice he had used for God. He had no awareness of how he had sounded. We fixed a time to start talking about how he saw God.

One reason why we neglect to look after ourselves as we serve is that we lose sight of our identity as children of God. Another reason is that we lose sight of God. That may seem impossible. After all, it is God we are serving. But the disturbing danger is that we can lose our focus on God even in the act of serving him. Focus is a good word, because even when we do not lose sight of God altogether, we can find our image of him becomes distorted.

Consider the elder brother in the parable of the lost son (Luke 15). Jesus told the story as a challenge to those who had lost sight both of their own need of God and of the nature of God as gracious Father. At the story's end, we meet the bitter elder son, angry at his younger brother's welcome. He reveals his lost focus on his father in these words: 'All these years I've been slaving for you…' (v. 29). Years of service had turned his father from loving parent to slave driver in his eyes.

You may recognise this loss of focus in your own life. I can tell it is happening to me when I connect the language of 'must', 'ought' and 'have to' with items on my to-do list.

What is our image of God – not just what we think it 'ought' to be, but the image of God which is revealed by our behaviour and language?

And who is this God we serve? A celestial watchmaker who has wound us up, set us going and now retreated into an uncaring distance? An angry tyrant who is always demanding more than we have to give? Is God a harsh judge for whom even our best is never quite good enough? Is he a kindly, old man, who smiles indulgently over our efforts but offers no real input?

The list could go on. This is important work, because our image of God and our sense of identity are closely entwined. They impact on how we present ourselves to others. Brennan Manning says:

> Our image of God makes us. Eventually we become like the God we image. One of the most beautiful fruits of knowing God is a compassionate attitude towards ourselves. Healing our image of God heals our image of ourselves.[95]

Restoring to focus our image of God transforms our approach to ministry and the way we serve others. It builds the permission we need to be kind to ourselves. Distorted images of God drive the joy out of the way we serve. If our God is angry, we live in fear of getting it wrong. If he is never satisfied, we work beyond our capacity to try to win some credit. And, although you may think that could never be you, we need to be honest that we don't always even know what our subconscious image of God is.

Origins and influences

When I was eleven, I sat at the back of physics classes, indifferent to the subject and wondering how to make sense of the scrawl written on the board. One day my friend on the back row started a prank whereby I put on his glasses to see if the teacher noticed. The moment I put on the glasses the jumbled scrawl on the board became neatly formed words and formulae! When I stepped outside, green blobs I had passed by on my way in became trees with individual branches, twigs and leaves. A whole new world of possibility opened up to me, although I confess that understanding physics was never part of it.

Similarly, we may need help to reveal the extent that our image of God has become distorted, because it tends to happen over such an extended period of time that we fail to notice that it has happened.

Pause to reflect

Sheridan Voysey offers this exercise to help uncover our images of God. We ask:

- *Images* – What pictures come to your mind when you think of God? Is God a strong father, a consoling mother, an indulgent grandfather or a bully? Is God a companion, a policeman, a friend or a warrior? Do you imagine God as an artist, a builder, a king, a judge or something more impersonal like light, energy, wind or something else? Try writing down or sketching the images you associate with God.
- *Characteristics* – How would you describe God's character? Is God stern or merciful? Forgiving or punishing? Arbitrary or fair? Is God serious, compassionate, patient, angry, generous, vindictive or humorous?

• *Origins* – How have your ideas about God been shaped? What was your first experience of God? How old were you? Who was present? What image of God did you develop? How did this change in teenage years? What about today? What books, films, courses, crises, conversations, paintings or other stimuli have shaped the way you imagine God? To the degree that you can, trace each characteristic of God that you noted back to its origin.[96]

Restoring focus

Once I discovered my failing eyesight, I was soon wearing glasses, which I have needed ever since. Reflecting on our image of God is an exercise we need to undertake regularly, to discover whether our lenses need changing, until finally 'we shall see face to face. Now I know in part; then I shall know fully, even as I am fully known' (1 Corinthians 13:12).

Paul's famous passage on love ends: 'And now these three remain: faith, hope and love. But the greatest of these is love' (1 Corinthians 13:13). All our refocusing must bring us back to this focal point, which one day will become perfectly clear to us. In the meantime, we need corrections. Recently, my son returned from holiday and found that some of his photos were blurry. It was remarkable how running them through computer software could instantly bring the blurry images into focus. Sometimes this is what we need to do with our God image. When something jars in how we feel about God, when circumstances or busyness or fatigue cloud our vision, we need to run that image of God back through the correcting filter.

Crooked and straight sticks

One summer, I visited Pisa, with its famous leaning bell tower. I searched for the ideal spot to capture an image that would portray the tower in all its glory, including, of course, its lean. I found the best way to do that was to ensure that not only was the tower in the photograph, but also the cathedral itself, with its true vertical lines. To prove a stick is crooked, you need a straight stick.

Our straight stick to enable us to see where our vision of God has become crooked is the Bible. Scripture is full of reminders of the truths of God's nature. It's good to become familiar with passages that speak to us of God's enduring character and faithfulness.

A good starting place is God's name as revealed in scripture. The unique name for God is Yahweh, indicated in most Bibles whenever we find the name LORD. This name was specifically revealed to be a constant reminder of the covenant-keeping God who would set his people free from slavery. There are various ways to translate the Hebrew word, but all speak of God's constant, trustworthy character. I sometimes express it as, 'I am now who I always have been and who I always will be.'

Exodus 34:6–7 describes Yahweh as 'the compassionate and gracious God, slow to anger, abounding in love and faithfulness, maintaining love to thousands, and forgiving wickedness, rebellion and sin'. Walter Brueggemann describes this as 'a formulation so studied that it may be reckoned to be a classic, normative statement to which Israel regularly returned, meriting the label "creed"'.[97]

This early statement of faith in God's character contains five glorious attributes that describe the heart of Israel's belief. Somehow, against all the odds and unlike their neighbours, for whom the gods were generally remote and frightening, Israel experienced a God who was *compassionate*, *gracious*, *abounding in love*, tenaciously *faithful* and *forgiving*. This character of God stands firm as the dynamic centre of their entire belief system, the straight stick to reveal their crooked god images. Like all spiritual mystery, it seems to be endlessly generative and fruitful, culminating in the full-blown, and practically incredible, concept of grace.

Of course, we do not twist the focus ring so far the other way that the focus is lost in the other direction. Our God is holy, a consuming fire, creator of all and worthy of all worship. However, the repeated message of scripture is that the God who lives in self-giving, fully-loving relationship for all eternity within the Trinity has taken extraordinary steps to invite us into this relationship and share in that intimacy. He wishes nothing – including our fears and distortions – to get in the way of that.

The Academy Award-winning film *Babette's Feast* (dir. Gabriel Axel, 1987) is a glorious parable of God's grace. Two sisters, together with others in their religious community, have found their hard-working lives of service have made them cold in their duty. They welcome Babette, a refugee, into their home, allowing her to work as a servant. Finally, Babette puts on such a generous feast, by way of expressing her gratitude, that the lives of the whole community are challenged and changed forever. As the feast ends, one of the guests makes this speech:

> There comes a time when our eyes are opened and we come to realise that mercy is infinite. We need only await it with confidence and receive it with gratitude. Mercy imposes no conditions. Everything we have chosen has been granted to us. And everything we rejected has also been granted… For mercy and truth have met together, and righteousness and bliss shall kiss one another.

Sometimes we only rediscover this holding together of the true nature of God alongside our core identity through an experience of falling, whatever that may look like. Richard Rohr writes:

> One of the only ways God can get us to let go of our private salvation project is some kind of suffering… I don't know anything else strong enough to force us to let go of our ego. Somehow our game has to fall apart. However, we've defined ourselves as successful, moral, right, good… has to fail. For

that is the only path toward your True Self, where you don't need to prove yourself to God anymore. It's not what you do for God; it's what God has done for you. You switch from trying to love God to just letting God love you. And it's at that point you fall in love with God.[98]

Pause to reflect

- Spend time with a passage of scripture that speaks of God's character, such as Psalm 103 or Isaiah 55.
- Make this poem by Edwina Gateley your prayer:

Let Your God Love You

Be silent.
Be still.
Alone.
Empty
Before your God.
Say nothing.
Ask nothing.
Be silent.
Be still.
Let your God look upon you.
That is all.
God knows.
God understands.
God loves you
With an enormous love,
And only wants
To look upon you
With that love.
Quiet.
Still.
Be.

Let your God –
Love you.[99]

6

A QUESTION OF BALANCE

Unhealthy ministry

Even when we know who we are and who God is, we can still often end up with lives that are out of balance. It is informative that the dominant symptom I experienced when heading towards burnout was extreme dizziness. Perhaps I should have questioned more readily whether my life and ministry were in balance!

Here's a poem by Edwina Gateley on the subject whose challenge I need to hear:

Balance

So much struggling –
realising that I need a balance
between reaching out and reaching in –
I need to do some things just for me,
like paint and play, and read and build sandcastles.
I need to stop – for a long time – to think about that.

Where did I miss it? Lose it?
For joy is the centre of ministry.
Joy should precede ministry,
nurture it and fulfil it
But I am so intense about ministry,
and take it so solemnly (as if I were responsible for it)
that I become weighed down
by its ups and downs,

its disappointments and failures.
I suffocate joy with seriousness…
I imagine everything depends on me –
when everything is God's business,
and God has already taken care of
all her creation and all her people.

We are only to walk with each other,
be with each other, love each other.
God's is the healing – the growing – and the fulfilling.
When I lose perspective
and imagine everything (or most things)
revolving round myself,
I make myself a little god,
and lose my joy.

For I was never made
to be a little god – only
to be loved by the Great God.
Perhaps I am too busy
trying to love other people
instead of learning to love myself.
When I can do that
I might begin to understand
how great God's love is.

When I go through
darkness, heaviness and anxiety,
it is God's invitation for me to stop
looking outwards
and start looking inwards
and be loving and gentle with myself.

I am called to minister
for my own joy.
When my joy diminishes

so does my ministry.
When I have fun and enjoy myself, God does!
Then I am most like God… who is joy![100]

You may recognise how an out-of-balance life squeezes joy out of ministry. You may yearn to find the place of balance. With a stronger permission to self-care, a deeper understanding of our core identity as God's children and a clearer view of the character of God, we are free to consider how we might find the way back to balance in ministry.

As we set off in a new direction, we need to be aware that the world is not on our side. Our society often drives us to the extremes of activity and velocity. Everything about our modern-day world is noisier, faster, more immediate than it has ever been before, and we feel its impact upon us.

Meyer Friedman describes this impact as 'Hurry Sickness': 'a continuous and unremitting attempt to accomplish more and more things… in less and less time, frequently in the face of opposition, real or imagined, from other people.'[101] This sickness has the disturbing nature of being highly contagious while also having the curious side effect that the sick think they are well, while those without the disease are given the impression that there is something wrong with them. As the Red Queen in *Through the Looking-Glass* explains, 'It takes all the running you can do to keep in the same place. If you want to go somewhere else, you must run at least twice as fast as that.'[102]

A scan of the symptoms of this contemporary disease brings the reality of this epidemic to the forefront.

Becoming easily irritated by how long daily activities take, like brushing teeth or boiling a kettle. My electric toothbrush has a two-minute timer. That's not very long in the greater scheme of things, and an early indicator that my life is too rushed is when that two minutes seems to be too long, and I do not complete the cycle, as if too much of my precious day would be taken up with the task.

Making decisions based on trying to beat time. Hurry Sickness causes us to switch lanes on the motorway or scan supermarket queues to assess which one will waste least time. I am embarrassed to confess the amount of satisfaction I get when I 'beat' the scheduled ETA suggested by my SatNav.

In the 2017 film *Wonder Woman* (dir. Patty Jenkins) there is a humorous illustration of this slavery to time as the eponymous heroine encounters the contemporary world. Here is an exchange between Diana and her fellow protagonist, Steve:

Diana: What is that?
Steve: That is a watch.
Diana: What does it do?
Steve: It tells the time. It tells you when to sleep, to eat –
Diana: That tiny thing tells you what to do?

Another sign of Hurry Sickness is when we *multitask* whenever possible – watching TV while checking emails and keeping up with the football scores. Many people would not dream of going anywhere or doing anything without lining up some music or podcasts to listen to.

Allied to this is the tendency to fill our life and house with *time-saving gadgets*, which ironically don't seem to have bought us that much time at all.

Those are the most immediate presenting symptoms, but a closer 'Hurry Sickness check' reveals more disturbing symptoms too.

Superficiality has been described as the curse of our age. It is so easy to succumb to the temptation to exchange depth for breadth.

In this attitude of hurry, we find ourselves with a *reduced ability to love* as the pace of life makes us irritated with everyone and leaves us arriving home from work with nothing to give to the people who matter most.

And this brings with it a *loss of the sense of wonder at the world around us*. Instead, we take the easy option of indulging in non-demanding distractions, like TV, alcohol, game apps or social media.

In the light of this, we can find ourselves with a life out of balance. Peter Scazzero speaks from his own experience:

> Something was missing. Our hearts were shrinking. Church leadership had no joy and felt like a heavy burden... I secretly dreamed of retirement, and I was only in my mid-thirties... God was beginning to get my attention and seemed to be pushing me deeper and deeper into a pit at each turn.[103]

That might be a place we recognise but it is surely not a place we want to go. In the end, this is a question of simple maths. We cannot continually give out if we are never making time to take in. That's not what Jesus was promising when he spoke of streams of living water flowing from within. If we want the stream to continue to flow, we need to pay attention to our relationship with Jesus.

Scazzero has identified a number of signs of unhealthy spirituality. Two in particular relate to the ways in which we get out of balance in ministry:[104]

- *Doing* for *God instead of being* with *God* – We love to be productive. As a result, enjoying God's presence for its own sake feels like a luxury. The underlying lie we fall for is that things will fall apart if we don't hold them together. But work for God that is not nourished by a deep interior life with God will eventually be contaminated by ego, power, need of approval and buying into the wrong ideas of success. We become human doings not human beings. Our sense of worth and validation shift from God's unconditional love for us to our works and performance. The bottom line is that our activity for God can only flow from a life with God. We cannot give away what we do not possess. Balance is essential.

* *Living without limits* – Sometimes our lives portray the underlying belief that to be a good Christian, we can never say no and must go on giving without limits. The only alternative is to be labelled 'uncommitted' or 'selfish'. The guilt that this can generate leads to discouragement, disengagement from ministry and even disenchantment with faith. The alternative is to accept that we are not God and to live within our limits. The way we live sometimes suggests that we can solve every problem or control every area of ministry. When we live without acknowledging our limits, we don't take appropriate care of ourselves. We become frantic, exhausted, overloaded and hurried. Sometimes this becomes a pathway to failing and falling.

Inward and outward flow

The secret of sustaining ministry is simply this: there needs to be balance between what you give out and what you take in spiritually. This is not about avoiding genuine sacrificial commitment to God. It is to acknowledge that if we consistently give out more than we take in, then we will eventually run out, get dry, burn out or grind to a halt.

If you are to avoid this unwelcome outcome, you will need to know what things build you up and feed you and what things drain you and sap your energy. This is not about putting ministry on one side of the scales and leisure on the other. This is about recognising what is life-giving and balancing it with what is not – within the whole of life.

Some of the things I count as life-giving are: being still; structured prayer; worship; team meetings; reading; exercise; photography;

and the countryside. Other things I enjoy doing and am called to do, but which use up more of my energy, are: preparing talks; service leading; sorting out finances; and running meetings.

We do not always know ourselves well enough to understand this. I found, in my days of ever-increasing fatigue, that when time off came not only did I not have the energy to do anything re-creative, I didn't always know what would be re-creative for me in the first place.

Do you know what brings you life? One way to discover this is to imagine a scenario where everything in your diary for the next day is cancelled. The day has suddenly and serendipitously become free. How would you spend your time?

It is interesting how floored people can be by this question. One woman responded honestly: 'Even if I had spent today cleaning my house from top to bottom, if I found myself free tomorrow I would clean it again.' She quickly added, 'I'd better think about that, hadn't I?' A couple of years later, I asked her the question again. 'That's easy,' she replied. 'I would enjoy spending some relaxation time with my family.'

Because we are all different, we need to discover for ourselves what activities are more life-giving than life-draining for us. For example, when visiting members of our community, it is possible to leave some visits feeling empty whereas we leave others feeling we have received more than given out. We could respond to this experience by organising our visiting schedule so that we balance a couple of the more draining visits with a beautifully life-giving one.

A recent conversation with a colleague illustrated this point well. She had been offered two new roles and was trying to discern which to take on. 'When I was offered the first role,' she said, 'my response was, yes, that's probably something I ought to be doing; it fits with my experience and training. But then the second opportunity came along, and as soon as it was offered I said, "Ooh, I'd like to do that."'

As she pondered the difference between her 'ought' and her 'ooh', the decision became clear.

This is not about choosing fun tasks at the expense of hard work. It is about discerning which tasks enable you to flourish in the long run. Ignatius of Loyola teaches this, using the language of 'consolation' – the life-giving ('ooh') stuff that draws us closer to God – as opposed to 'desolation' – the life-taking stuff that leads us away from God. Sometimes we know it is the hard choice that draws us close to God and so, costly though it is, it is still consolation. Conversely, the apparently more attractive opportunity might feel like it would be a place of consolation, but we discern that it would lead us further from God and his purposes.

Of course, if we are going to become more skilled at this balanced living we will need to both know our limits and then be willing to set the boundaries that enable us to keep within them. This too is a self-care issue. Brené Brown recognises that, for most of us, the moment someone asks us to do something is fraught with vulnerability. To answer yes may often seem like the easiest way out, but it comes at a price of feeling resentful immediately afterwards. She sums up the dilemma: 'Daring to set boundaries is about having the courage to love ourselves, even when we risk disappointing others.'[105] We can't base our own worthiness on others' approval. Only when we believe, deep down, that we are enough can we say, 'Enough!'

In order to help us grow in boundary-setting Brown suggests these three steps:

- *Make a mantra* – We need something to remind us of our need to set compassionate boundaries, especially in that moment when a request hangs in the air. Before making a response, Brown silently repeats, 'Choose discomfort over resentment.'
- *Keep a resentment journal* – When we hear ourselves internally resenting a person or task, recording that helps us notice what is going on and what are the sources of our 'task resentment'.

- *Rehearse* – Because saying no can be so hard, we may need to rehearse saying aloud, 'I can't take that on,' or, 'I'm sorry I can't help on this occasion.' Boundary-setting needs practice.[106]

If we are to move in this direction of balance and to live within our limits, we will need to put some tasks down, including some that have been added to the leader's to-do list over the years. Karl Vaters says:

> Pastors were never meant to carry this big a burden. No one person is capable of being the preacher, teacher, vision-caster, CEO, leader, evangelist, soul-winner, fundraiser, marriage counsellor, and all-around paragon of virtue that we expect pastors to pull off.[107]

Some will need to say no to the unreasonable expectations of church members, leadership structures and denominational officials. But all of us need to say no to our own unbiblical expectations of ourselves. We are not the builders of the church. We are not capable of working ourselves to the bone emotionally and spiritually without something breaking inside us.

I am very blessed to have a 'boss' over my church-based ministry who believes in seeking the life-giving. When we discuss my contribution to church life, he invites me to choose what is life-giving. This gives me the freedom not to join in with some things I used to do or feel I ought to do. It enables me to opt in to areas where I can offer something really helpful. This is incredibly generous, but it is also very wise, because when I offer ministry which is life-giving to me, then it will also be life-giving to those to whom it is offered.

As I reflect on this I am reminded that even though this extraordinary generosity may be unusual within the church, it is found first in the God who made us, gifted us, called us and sends us out to do his work in such a way that, being blessed, we become, and remain, a blessing to many.

Pause to reflect

- Ask yourself, 'What sort of people, activities and tasks drain you? Which bring life?'
- Consider what the balance is between your inflow and your outflow.
- List these in two columns and consider how balanced your life is.
- Do you know what your limits are? Do they need adjusting for new circumstances, or because you are you and not someone else you are competing with?
- Finally, consider this wisdom from Winnie the Pooh:

'Say, Pooh, why aren't you busy?' I said.
'Because it's a nice day,' said Pooh.
'Yes, but –'
'Why ruin it?' he said.
'But you could be doing something Important,' I said.
'I am,' said Pooh.
'Oh? Doing what?'
'Listening,' he said.
'Listening to what?'
'To the birds. And that squirrel over there.'
'What are they saying?' I asked.
'That it's a nice day,' said Pooh.
'But you know that already,' I said.
'Yes, but it's always good to hear that somebody else thinks so, too,' he replied.[108]

Is this the end of the line?

This awareness of who we are and what we need is vital, because the impact of getting it wrong is so serious for us as individuals; for our families and friends; for our churches; and for the kingdom of God.

The statistics are disturbing. In 2016, the Francis Schaeffer Institute published research on clergy health and stress.[109] Although 90% reported feeling honoured to be a pastor, the underlying figures reveal the huge demands on those in ministry. Indeed, it is this commitment itself that makes it harder first to notice and then to respond to the pressure. However, a failure to respond leaves us facing breakdown.

The study found 54% of pastors were working over 55 hours a week, with 43% describing themselves as overstressed; 57% couldn't pay their bills without a second income; and nearly a quarter felt distanced from their families. In a previous survey[110] 77% of pastors felt their marriage was not good, while a quarter of leaders' families reported resenting the church. Nearly 20% confessed to being tempted to start or actually starting an inappropriate relationship.

It is not surprising then that 26% of leaders were overly fatigued; 28% were spiritually undernourished; 35% battled with depression; and 9% described themselves as burnt out.[111]

Behind the statistics are real people seeking to fulfil God's call with obedience and passion, yet finding themselves under extraordinary pressure. A young minister described the public criticism endured at a leaders' meeting as 'like being bludgeoned around the head with a baseball bat!' As he took in the violence of that imagery, he began to realise why he felt physically drained and spiritually empty, and was fantasising about escape.

In a Church of England General Synod debate on the emotional health of clergy in 2017, Justin Welby said, 'The hardest work I have ever done, and the most stressful, was as a parish priest. It was isolated, insatiably demanding, and I was, on the whole, working without colleagues. That wears people down.'

In the same debate, Yvonne Warren, a Christian psychotherapist married to a clergyman, declared, 'I have a real concern about all that is expected of our clergy... in the work that we're asking them to do... In my work as a therapist I'm finding many clergy are burnt out... [and] suffer from mental-health issues, with families at the end of their tether and many clergy going off sick.'[112]

A recent *Church Times* article brings home the impact on families:

> I am writing anonymously about my mental-health breakdown as a clergy partner in a difficult parish, where the forces of stress, poor supervision, and impossible expectations imposed on my husband travelled through me... Such was the severity of the knocks, and the capriciousness of the systems set up to support him, that I cracked under the strain, and my mental well-being was sent into chaos.[113]

I have been poked in the chest by an angry parishioner and physically backed into a corner by a group of (generally very gentle) people who disagreed with a decision. Handwritten letters arriving through the letterbox become a fearsome event, and, of course, the proliferation of email means a leader can switch on the computer to find an inbox full of criticism and complaint marked by a hostility reflective of the trolling that social media appears to have made prevalent. Another weary leader, from whom I had never previously heard a hint of coarse language, cried out in desperation, 'Do we really have to put up with this s**t?'

All this begs the question, 'How do I know if I am heading towards the end of the line?'

You don't wake up one morning and suddenly have burnout. It creeps up on you over time. However, our bodies and minds do give us warnings, and if you know what to look for you can before it's too late recognise whether this is a temporary blip or a cul-de-sac.

Sherrie Bourg Carter describes burnout as a state of chronic stress that leads to physical and emotional exhaustion, cynicism and detachment, and feelings of ineffectiveness and lack of accomplishment.[114] Each of these areas has its own symptoms that exist along a continuum. In other words, the difference between stress and burnout is a matter of degree, which means that the earlier you recognise the signs, the better able you will be to avoid burnout, provided that you do something to address the symptoms when you recognise them.

Physical and emotional exhaustion

Chronic fatigue is a tiredness that does not fade with rest, at least in the short run. Initially you feel a daily lack of energy. In later stages, you can feel physically and emotionally depleted, with a sense of dread for the day ahead. You move along the continuum from having trouble sleeping once or twice a week through to nightly insomnia. To go to bed exhausted and yet not be able to sleep is hugely frustrating, and it leaves many dark hours to feel the dread of another demanding day on an empty tank.

Additional physical symptoms include chest pain, heart palpitations, shortness of breath, gastrointestinal pain, loss of appetite, dizziness, fainting, headaches and poor concentration. You may suffer from a compromised immune system rendering you vulnerable to infections. Many people in stressful professions become ill every time they take a holiday. These symptoms should all be checked by a doctor. Remember, your body does not lie, so it may be these physical symptoms that sound the first warning that a response is needed.

Alongside the physical symptoms, anxiety becomes an unwelcome companion. It begins with mild tension, but it has the potential to develop into a paralysing anxiety that interferes with your work and personal life. Accompanying feelings of sadness or tearfulness may run alongside a simmering anger.

Carrying all this renders us prone to depression. At first, you may feel mildly sad or occasionally hopeless, with accompanying feelings of guilt and worthlessness. Ultimately, you may feel trapped, severely depressed and think the world would be better off without you. This is most definitely a time to seek immediate professional help.

Cynicism and detachment

These feelings begin with mild loss of enjoyment, discouraging us from doing the extra miles, before moving on through pessimism and then towards the desire to escape. Finally, loss of enjoyment can extend to all areas of life, including the desire to socialise.

What starts with reluctance to grab a coffee with a colleague may end up with feelings of rage when the phone or doorbell rings. You may start coming to work early or leaving late to avoid interactions, so that disengagement develops into isolation.

In this place of cynical detachment and isolation, we are more prone than usual to temptation, as we are drawn to take the edge off negative feelings with alcohol or other substances. We may look for fake intimacy through inappropriate relationships or pornography. We may plunge ourselves into debt through uncontrolled 'retail therapy'.

Feelings of ineffectiveness and lack of accomplishment

Added to the sense of apathy and hopelessness are feelings of ineffectiveness and lack of accomplishment. We develop a general sense that nothing is going right and nothing matters. We ask, 'What's the point?' Feeling ineffective adds fuel to existing irritability, interfering with personal and professional relationships. At its worst, relationships and careers can be destroyed.

A vicious circle is formed as lack of productivity and poor performance take hold in spite of long hours worked. It feels like running up a downwards escalator that accelerates however much we ourselves speed up.

If you're not experiencing any of these problems, that's great! However, the warning signs are offered as a means of preventing the insidious creature that is burnout from creeping up on you as you live your busy life.

In summary, you need to pay attention to three things:

- Your *body*, which will never lie and may be the early warning siren for burnout.
- Your *language*, when it becomes littered with greater negativity, burden or anger than you normally express.
- Your *relationships*, when they begin to hit rocky ground. We may need a partner or trusted friend to alert us, because they may notice the severity of our symptoms before we do.

If any of this sounds too familiar to you, this is a wake-up call that you are on a dangerous path. Find time to honestly assess the amount of stress in your life, and find ways to reduce it before it's too late. Burnout isn't like the flu. It won't just pass by, unless you make changes in your life. As hard as that may seem, it is the wisest thing to do, because making a few changes now will keep you in the race with plenty of fuel to get across the finish line.

And even as we notice these signs, we can return to the truths of our identity and of God's character. We remember that we are fragile vessels but loved by God nevertheless. We discover in a deeper way the paradox of realising our ultimate worth in God's eyes through recognising our ultimate unworthiness in the sense of what we bring to the table.

The Velveteen Rabbit is a children's novel about a toy rabbit learning about love and what it means to become real, reflecting our own pilgrimage to embrace our authentic selves. Here, the Skin Horse explains the process of becoming real to the young Velveteen Rabbit:

'Real isn't how you are made,' said the Skin Horse. 'It's a thing that happens to you. When a child loves you for a long, long time, not just to play with, but REALLY loves you, then you become Real.'

'Does it hurt?' asked the Rabbit.

'Sometimes,' said the Skin Horse, for he was always truthful. 'When you are Real you don't mind being hurt.'

'Does it happen all at once, like being wound up,' he asked, 'or bit by bit?'

'It doesn't happen all at once,' said the Skin Horse. 'You become. It takes a long time. That's why it doesn't happen often to people who break easily, or have sharp edges, or who have to be carefully kept. Generally, by the time you are Real, most of your hair has been loved off, and your eyes drop out and you get loose in the joints and very shabby. But these things don't matter at all, because once you are Real you can't be ugly, except to people who don't understand.'[115]

Pause to reflect

- How real do you feel right now?
- Review the signs of burnout and honestly assess where you stand.
- Check this out with someone you trust.
- Is there any immediate action you need to take?

The forgotten commandment

Reintegration through the practice of looking after ourselves is an urgent matter if we take seriously the degree to which those in all forms of ministry can feel stressed, fatigued or discouraged. Those on the slippery slope towards burnout need to put the brakes on somehow. Here is a surprising way to do that:

Start keeping the sabbath.

I wonder if the fourth commandment (Exodus 20:8) is the one most frequently broken by God's most faithful people. It has become the forgotten commandment. The busyness that infects both world and church has squeezed out the practice of sabbath rest so that, if we think about it at all, it is merely as another task to fit into our busy schedule – and to feel guilty about when we don't!

We can tell sabbath matters to God simply by its inclusion in the ten commandments. When God distilled these rules for living into a top ten, one precious place in that list went to sabbath-keeping. It is not an optional extra for the super holy or the totally un-busy. Jesus challenged attitudes to it, but only because people had lost sight of how the sabbath was God's gift, not because he thought it was wrong.

How would you complete this sentence: 'I'll have a rest when…'? The answers people have given me are revealing. One leader answered, 'I'll have a rest when the church is exactly how Jesus would have it be.' He then realised he might have quite a wait. His response reveals the pressure upon us due to the urgency of the task of mission, but also that it was time for him to learn that he might be living without limits.

This attitude doesn't necessarily change automatically over time. Another response is 'when all the jobs are done', but I know many who are still waiting for that illusory moment to arrive even into later years. Many have been set patterns of hard work by the generations before them which remain a strong influence. One person told how whenever she gives herself permission to rest, these words of her mother come forcibly into her mind: 'The devil makes work for idle hands.'

Others respond, 'I'll rest when I'm too tired to carry on; when I realise I need it; when the children go to school or leave home.' Rock icon Bruce Springsteen confesses, 'At rest I was not at ease and to be at ease I could not rest.'[116]

One reason we have dwelt on identity is that if we are to choose 'being' over 'doing', we have to be content with who we are. Any discomfort, shame or uncertainty with self forces us back to the escape of doing. Busyness anaesthetises us from any discomfort at intimacy with self or God, and Christian busyness even more so, because it promises a worthiness of its own to compensate for our lack. We can thus fall into one of two categories in our relationship with work and rest. Some find themselves hiding in rest due to an insecurity about work that prevents them from getting on with it. Others work from a place of insecurity about rest that makes it feel like forbidden fruit. The healthy and balanced goal is to be able to both work and rest from a place of security about who we are.

Unfinished business

We are not helped in this by society's obsession with getting things finished. In England, the delayed completion of the new Wembley Stadium became a source of national shame. However, the great counter to this prevailing value is both a magnificent work of art and a place of worship: the Sagrada Familia in Barcelona. This remarkable edifice is an inspiration to millions. The surprise is that even though construction began in 1882, it is still not finished. Architect Antoni Gaudí devoted his life to the project, yet when he died in 1926 less than a quarter of it was complete. Construction only passed the midpoint in 2010 and, with the greatest challenges remaining, the current anticipated completion date is 2026. Nobody is holding their breath on this, but neither are they losing sleep. Part of this building's magnificence is in its very unfinished-ness. Each generation accepts what they inherit and makes their contribution to pass on to the next. All are able to see God's glory in its current state of being a work in progress. The Sagrada Familia models what it is to work with passion towards an end without necessarily seeing the final product. Gaudí knew from the beginning that the vision God had given him was bigger than he could complete. He was okay with that, insisting, 'My client is not in a hurry.'

I was long attracted by this idea of a building which could be unfinished and yet still beautiful and glorifying to God. The moment when I finally walked into that vast and unique worship space, in my own unfinished-ness, was a profoundly moving and inspiring experience.

This prayer, honouring Oscar Romero and taken from a homily written by Ken Untener in 1979, describes what it means to live in an unfinished kingdom. It was quoted by Pope Francis in 2015.

It helps now and then to step back and take a long view.
The Kingdom is not only beyond our efforts, it is beyond our
    vision.
We accomplish in our lifetime only a fraction of the magnificent
    enterprise that is God's work.
Nothing we do is complete,
which is another way of saying that the kingdom always lies
    beyond us.
No statement says all that could be said.
No prayer fully expresses our faith.
No confession brings perfection,
no pastoral visit brings wholeness.
No programme accomplishes the Church's mission.
No set of goals and objectives includes everything.

This is what we are about. We plant the seeds that one day will
    grow.
We water the seeds already planted knowing that they hold
    future promise.
We lay foundations that will need further development.
We provide yeast that produces effects far beyond our
    capabilities.

We cannot do everything,
and there is a sense of liberation in realising this.
This enables us to do something, and to do it very well.
It may be incomplete, but it is a beginning,

a step along the way,
an opportunity for the Lord's grace to enter and do the rest.
We may never see the end results,
but that is the difference between the master builder and the
    worker.

We are workers, not master builders, ministers, not messiahs.
We are prophets of a future not our own.[117]

Permission to stop?

From where will you get your permission to stop? It will not come
from completing a job that has no ending, from receiving affirmation
that seldom comes or from a hierarchical permission that rarely
exists. Instead, it will have to come from the self-love and self-care
of which we have spoken, augmented by obedience to the fourth
commandment, which is our permission to rest.

I was sad to hear someone working within church leadership ask,
'What if you believe in self-care and sabbath rest, but your employers
do not give you permission to honour those values?' Sometimes we
need to speak and live prophetically against the prevailing culture.
Significantly, Walter Brueggemann's book on this is entitled *Sabbath
as Resistance*. In it, he writes, 'In our own contemporary context of
the rat race of anxiety, the celebration of Sabbath is an act of both
resistance and alternative.'[118]

In Egypt, God's people lived as slaves to production, with constant
toil and no rest. God intervened to set his people free from this
slavery, setting this God apart from other gods. His resting on the
seventh day demonstrates that God is not a workaholic, anxious
about how creation will function without his activity.

It may not feel like it, but we have a choice between restlessness or
restfulness. The epidemic of restlessness infecting the world and the

church makes us think that we have to be permanently productive. We sometimes sanctify this by calling it the 'Protestant work ethic', and we are drawn inexorably into a consumerist world characterised by the restless acquisition of consumer goods and the abuse of creation itself.

Sabbath invites us to step outside of this restlessness. The command to remember the sabbath contains a permission to be 'other than' the world around us in a perhaps incomprehensible but ultimately winsome way. We could say that sabbath is God's antidote to workaholism – the escape ladder for men and women who have fallen into the trap of believing their personal worth is built upon what they do rather than who they are. Seen this way, sabbath isn't just a rest, it is a way of standing against acquisitiveness and competition and standing for compassion and justice. Brueggemann explains:

> On the Sabbath: you do not have to do more. You do not have to sell more. You do not have to control more. You do not have to know more. You do not have to have your kids in ballet or soccer. You do not have to be younger or more beautiful. You do not have to score more.[119]

To locate sabbath within the realm of resistance, however, reminds us that it will not come easily. It encourages us when we too find it is something we must fight for. Sabbath-keeping goes against the grain of society and of our own inner drives. But we may also discover the power of hearing this permission from God to join him in letting go of anxious, competitive restlessness in order to enter into the rest which is his promise and gift to us. Sabbath is taking time – time to be holy and time to be human.

Rest is something we do not give ourselves enough time to do. The second most common deathbed regret collated by a nurse working with terminally ill people, after the wish to live a life more true to themselves, is 'I wish I hadn't worked so hard.'[120]

Why do we resist the very thing to which so many people belatedly wish they had given more time? It is partly because of the identity issues and inner drives we have already described, those inner voices that make us feel that we always need to accomplish something. One spiritually hungry woman said to me, 'I feel God is calling me to spend time in stillness on retreat, so why do I feel it would be wasteful to give my time to something like that?' I wondered with her about where the need came from for her to be so productive that this felt more worthwhile than sabbath time with God.

God modelled rest for us in the creation narrative (Genesis 1). At the end of each day and at the end of the very first week, God stopped and saw creation's goodness. He didn't need to rest, but he chose to rest in order to set a pattern for us to follow. There are rhythms built into creation, and when we don't live with those rhythms things start to unravel. Why do we spend too much time in the church squeezing blood from stones? Vincent de Paul comments, 'It's a trick of the devil to incite good souls to do more than they are able, in order that they may no longer be able to do anything.'[121]

Stephen Covey advises, 'You have to decide what your highest priorities are and have the courage… to say "no" to other things. And the way you do that is by having a bigger "yes" burning inside.'[122] Can we allow sabbath to become the bigger 'yes' in us so that we can say 'no' to other good things in order to embrace the best?

Many of us affirm this new pattern in principle, but in practice always find a reason why it cannot start just yet. Like modern versions of the invitees in Jesus' parable of the great banquet (Luke 14:15–24), we offer numerous excuses why we must decline the invitation to this particular feast. We're launching a new programme; I've got the annual report to write; I'm seeing in some new staff; I've just lost my old staff; there's too much going on at the moment.

Sabbath principles

Further encouragement comes as we understand more deeply what sabbath is really about. Theologian Marva Dawn speaks of the impact of sabbath on her: 'Learning to keep an entire day as sabbath changed my life.'[123]

She notes that the creation narrative portrays the very first day for humankind as one of rest, not work. With the Jewish day beginning in the evening, God's pattern is that we eat, sleep and then work from a place of rest. It is we who have turned rest into an optional extra that we tag on when we have done all the other jobs or simply collapsed into a heap.

Dawn identifies four principles to reveal the true nature of sabbath.[124]

1 Sabbath is about ceasing

The root word of sabbath itself means to stop or cease. God knows that if we waited until we were finished, we would never stop, so he invites us to stop anyway. The foundation of sabbath is about stopping the endless striving that characterises much of everyday life. We can put tools away, turn off computers and let go of our many projects for self-improvement. We are freed on this one day from words like 'produce', 'accomplish' and 'achieve'. We can stop 'trying to be God' by our exhausting efforts to determine our own future. Instead, we pause to bask in God's acceptance of us for who we are, not what we do. We admit that we will never complete all the tasks, and we discover that the world continues just fine when we stop. Released from anxiety, we rest in the sovereignty of God, depending upon him for our needs. Sabbath-keeping therefore contains the key spiritual issue of trusting God enough to believe that he can manage without us. Not keeping sabbath may signal a lack of such trust.

Our lives are often so full that it feels as if there is no space to cease or even to be flexible. We plan back-to-back meetings and wonder why we are exhausted. When a pressing need or an exciting opportunity arises, we are already at full capacity. God's people were taught the principle of working with a margin – spare capacity around the edges, as with a field, so that those in need could glean from the edges.

Today, the margin is the vital space between your load and your limits. What would your life look like with more margins? Can you create margins for your emotional capacity, your physical limits or your financial resources? Both you and those around you could be blessed by your learning and choosing to cease before you reach the limits. I heard a leader recommend putting the word 'something' into the diary regularly. When someone calls on your time you can respond truthfully, 'I already have something in the diary.' This is a start, but could we reach a point when we can truthfully respond, 'I'm sorry, I need that space for myself'?

2 Sabbath is about resting

We need rest for our whole selves – spiritual, physical, relational and emotional. Rest marks out God's people as different. Can we find the courage to be noticed not for our lives of busyness but rather for our lives of balance between work and rest? God's people were freed from the need to fill time with work not because work was bad but because, uncontained, it takes over and captures the affections of the worker. So work loses its meaning and there is no time for worship or rest. To a nation of freed slaves, this command was God's permission not to enter into another kind of work-based slavery.

This rest is not another word for idleness nor for that new kind of busyness we call 'leisure'. Our leisure industry (note the tautology) is bigger than ever, yet there remains an epidemic of fatigue, indicating that we no longer understand genuine rest as distinct from the pursuit of leisure.

Pumping iron in the gym, undertaking the next triathlon, trekking in the Himalayas or even binge-watching the latest streaming TV series is not necessarily restful. We need a constructive re-creation that is centred upon God. And because we are all different, this will vary considerably. One person's rest is another's hard work. I know someone whose perfect day off involves digging his allotment. Others relax around a meal with friends, while some prefer a quiet walk in the countryside or playing in the garden with children. What matters – as with the inflow and outflow of ministry – is to find what is rest for you. Aesop's fable warns that a bow which is always bent will soon break.[125]

3 Sabbath is about embracing

Through rest, we embrace afresh gospel values and apply them to our lives. Being intentional about living the sabbath involves a grace that includes gifts of human intimacy and compassion. We may meet with others or display generosity – moving towards living simply so that others can simply live. Sabbath includes embracing our calling to live lives for God. We remember to whom we belong. We return to eternal truths.

Our world bombards us with demands upon our time and energy that speak more loudly than the still, small voice of God. Sabbath's pause enables us to discern more effectively how we will allocate our time and commitments. Sabbath is God's gift for recalibrating our lives as we remember what are (and what are not) the really important truths. We reflect upon where we have given our energy in the last week. What does it mean? Who did I do it for? How well did I do it? Why did I do it? This reintroduces meaning into our work. In the long run, it may point to new directions that we might otherwise not see as we rush from week to week and task to task. Tony Horsfall says:

> Stopping is pausing for a few minutes, a few hours, or a few days, to remember who I am, why I am here, and to receive strength for the next part of the journey. So, stopping is a positive activity, it is not about doing nothing.[126]

We need to question whether our churches give permission for people to embrace sabbath. Or are they just another place of busyness? Someone once said of their church Sunday, 'I'm glad we only have one day of rest each week. I don't think I could survive any more like this!'

4 Sabbath is about feasting and celebration

Sabbath is, above all, celebratory. We anticipate the eschatological party through our weekly celebration. This is very different from historical experiences of sabbath as a day of prohibitions. It is there not to exclude fun and joy but to allow for it. It may include worship, music, food, beauty, community, conversation, joy, wonder, delight and play. It may be a time to enjoy, rather than rush past, creation; to savour, not gobble down, food; to use our senses as we move more slowly; and even to be willing to be interrupted by conversation.

Those of us serving in churches know that Sundays do not usually work as sabbath days, especially if our involvement is considerable. Another day in the week needs to fulfil this sabbath purpose. While it is demanding to find this time, the benefits are enormous. In the meantime, you could include mini-sabbaths within each day, giving yourself time for these sabbath practices, even for five minutes at a time.

Pause to reflect

- Plan a sabbath day that is full of delight and permission, not rules and regulations (or work).
- What would need to change to make that possible for you?
- Experiment and adjust as you find out what works for you.

This chapter has been about restoring some sense of balance to lives that have become unbalanced by 'good reasons', such as our desire to serve, our awareness of the needs around us and our response to God's call. Our lives may also have become unbalanced by our semiconscious serving of our inner drives, by our distorted images of God or by our lack of self-awareness or understanding of what is life-giving for us. The outcome of an unbalanced ministry will be emptiness and ultimately burnout with damaging impacts. But now, with sabbath restored as God's gift to us, we can begin to see how we might keep on loving and serving in the long run with a ministry that is genuinely sustainable, fruitful and even joyful. Finally, having taken the risk of giving ourselves permission to self-care, we may be ready to consider partaking of some soul food.

7

SOUL FOOD

At the heart of the relationship between God and his people, you will often find food. Many Jewish traditions are rich with celebration and enjoyment of feasting. Isaiah issues this wonderful invitation: 'Come, all you who are thirsty… you who have no money, come, buy and eat! Come, buy wine and milk without money and without cost… Listen, listen to me, and eat what is good, and you will delight in the richest of fare' (Isaiah 55:1–2).

This chapter offers practical ways to take basic self-care into the realm of the indulgent, to sustain us for the journey ahead. Here is both a real feast and a good diet, which is about taking in healthy food rather than junk! I call it soul food. In England, this is food for a wintry day that really warms you up – soups and stews come to mind as the wind blows the leaves from the trees outside my window.

The term 'soul food' originally derives from the southern states of the USA and refers back to the food eaten by enslaved Africans. So it also references impoverished people eating the best they can. As the term grew, it spoke not only of taste, goodness and home-cooked sustenance but also of all that goes with it when we gather to eat together, such as community, rootedness and laughter.

Join me now as we work our way through a feast to feed your soul throughout your long and fruitful ministry.

Starter: slowing down

We begin with slowing down. This connects with the teaching about sabbath. If we are to cease, we first need to slow down, otherwise the shock at departing from our full-speed-ahead lifestyle may be too much.

In one of her first sermons, my young friend Laura bravely proclaimed these words: 'God loves you. God loves you. God loves you. Can you hear that? If not, slow down and listen!'

At our usual fast pace, everything is harder to notice or hear, but nothing more so than the gentle whisper of God's 'I love you.' The same is true in caring for others. We cannot effectively offer support while our mind is preoccupied. Have you tried talking with someone who constantly glances at their watch? Eugene Peterson asks, 'How can I lead people into the quiet place beside still waters if I am in perpetual motion?'[127]

Skye Jethani warns:

> As a young church leader… I hear a lot about… sprinting. Who is calling us to sit down and take our time? How many burned-out… young men and women would still be in ministry if they had heard this countercultural message?…
>
> As our pace slows from a sprint, to a walk, to a limp we come to a richer understanding of our calling and identity. We slow down enough to experience God's presence in our lives.[128]

John Ortberg speaks of the influence of Dallas Willard on his slowing down: 'The remarkable characteristic of his body was how unhurried it was. Someone said of him once: "I'd like to live in his time zone."' This conversation between the two illustrates Willard's approach:

John: What must I do to stay spiritually healthy?

Dallas: You must ruthlessly eliminate hurry from your life.

John: Right, got that. What else?

Dallas: There is nothing else. Hurry is the greatest enemy of the spiritual life in our day. You must ruthlessly eliminate hurry from your life.[129]

Sometimes the thought of slowing down brings not only anxiety about how we will get things done, but a deeper fear of what life would be like if it was not filled with the distraction of busyness. Chef Marco Pierre White confessed, 'My work was a painkiller – it was where I hid.'[130]

My illness-enforced slowing down has transformed my daily walk. Previously I walked everywhere briskly, but when illness slowed me down, I started noticing things around me: the buds forming on the trees in spring; the rise and fall of the river level; the wild flowers among the meadow grass; the people I passed regularly on my circuit; even, as a real sign of grace, a glimpse of a kingfisher perched on a branch.

At this slow pace, I was drawn to God in ways never previously encountered. I have wept at the sight of a rose, felt my heart sing at the way sunlight illuminates a leaf, and even rejoiced that the bowing of my head in fatigue brought into view a wren darting into the hedgerow.

This 'starter' of slowing down also developed for me into other ways of seeing. From being a very wordy person, I became more open to image and imagination. Stripped of the ability to read, photography became an interest. As I began to read again I became a slower reader. I get through fewer books, but I take in more of what I read.

God has built hundreds of natural pauses into our bodies every day. They are the essential pauses that separate our breathing in from our breathing out. Taking a moment to notice and to use those natural pauses in itself causes you to slow down. Try it and notice what you can now hear, what you can see around you that you might not otherwise have noticed.

A soul-food feast begins with this choice to slow down. Busyness inhibits the reflection needed to sustain a life of love with God and others. Slowing down is actually a way to increase the inward flow that will create balance within your life and give you something to offer.

When 'being' and 'doing' get out of balance, we end up off-centre. Our serving for God can only properly flow from a life with God. We need to create an easy familiarity with God's presence at work, rest and play. This requires that we slow down to pay attention. Our goal is to love God with our whole being – to be conscious of God through our daily life so that, whether we are stopped or active, we know his presence with us.

What an impact that could have on those around us. Monica Furlong writes:

> I am clear what I want of the clergy. I want them to be people who can, by their own happiness and contentment, challenge my ideas about status, success, money, and teach me how to live more independently of such drugs. I want them to be people who can dare… to refuse to work flat out… to be secure enough in the value of what they are doing to have time to read, to sit and think, and who can face the emptiness and possible depression which often attack people when they do not keep the surface of their mind occupied… I want them to be people who can sit still without feeling guilty, and from whom I can learn some kind of tranquillity in a society which has almost lost the art.[131]

Unless we make slowing down a deliberate act, it just won't happen. David speaks of the shepherd who *makes us* lie down in green pastures and actively *leads us* by still waters (Psalm 23:2). Instead, we rush through the green pastures without being nourished and fail to notice the beauty of quiet waters in our desire to get from A to B.

Personally, I need time each day to pay attention to what is happening within me and bring it to God. Rather than mask this with busyness, I need space to explore feelings and wrestle with emotions. Slowing down has encouraged me to pay attention to what is going on inside – the reasons I do things, the ways in which I am or am not free. I'm getting under the surface to examine the iceberg beneath.

At my greatest pace, I would have described myself as committed and obedient rather than needy and driven. I have now learned of my inner drive not to let people down; my tendency to put myself well down the priority list; the missed meals, delayed toilet visits and working on through stress to distress. At the time, it all seemed easier than actually slowing down. My enforced stop gave me the level of desperation as well as the time needed to take a good, long, hard look within. I've needed the help of an experienced therapist to unpack why I do the things I do and feel the things I feel, and how the roots of some of this behaviour go back to the very earliest stages of my life and feed into how I gain my sense of identity. I'm not sure I would have given that much time and effort to this process without the requirement to slow down.

Now that I have more choice of pace, I resist hurriedness by setting apart specific times for silent prayer – without words, simply being still in the presence of God. My day begins with making the choice to slow down. It is a mini-sabbath in which I lay down the need to have a godlike control over and responsibility for everything. Instead I remake my own connection with who I am in God. Ideally, I do this as part of my morning prayer time, along with using liturgy, Bible reading and intercessory prayer. When I can, I follow that up at lunchtime with a short walk consciously in the presence of God. It reminds me of God walking in the garden with Adam and Eve. Walking is something you do with someone you care about – it's not the walk that counts, it's the being with the other person. And on this walk, I deliberately stop for a moment at a point early on to remind me that this walk is a slowing down and turning away from the frenzy of work. In that moment or two of stopping, I make myself aware of the presence of God and invite him to continue to make me aware of his presence through the rest of the day. It turns a power walk into a Power Walk!

Pause to reflect

- How would you describe the 'time zone' you live in? How would others describe it?
- Indulging in this starter begins with one tiny subversive step. What might that be for you?

Main course: feasting on the love of God

After the starter comes the main course of feasting extravagantly on the unfailing love of God. Christianity is more about God's relentless pursuit of us than ours of him. That's not always how we live, but as we start by slowing down and turning aside from frenzied activity, we experience God's love afresh. As Martin Laird writes, 'Not only has this God we desire already found us... but God has never not found us.'[132]

Jesus' lost-and-found parables declare that God's inexhaustible love always celebrates our return to him. However, transferring this knowledge from head to heart is fraught with obstacles, so we need actively to pull up our chair to this feast-laden table.

We battle with our sense of worthiness to attend such a feast. Negative internal voices whisper, 'I'm a mistake or worthless. I'm not allowed to fail. I need the approval of certain people to feel okay. I don't have the right to experience joy. I'm not allowed to say what I feel. I'm valued for what I do not for who I am.'

Many deeply committed Christians recognise themselves in statements like these. Like the prodigal, we consider ourselves more hired hand than loved sons and daughters. We need a renewed insight into 'how wide and long and high and deep is the love of Christ' (Ephesians 3:18), so that we may be grounded in our true identity as deeply loved children of God.

Sometimes we only rediscover these truths at rock bottom. At a low point of my journey I was on retreat but struggling to engage. I entered the chapel and found a poster of Rembrandt's *The Return of the Prodigal Son* (c. 1668). Gazing at this image while being confronted with my own total bankruptcy, I felt a new identification with the rag-wearing, head-shaven, bare-footed beggar. I too fell to my knees and allowed myself to feel the gracious arms of the loving Father welcoming me home, just as I was, and inviting me to a celebration feast.

Ministry is transformed when we are able to operate out of this sense of being known and loved by God. We all need to find our own times and means to feast at this table and gorge ourselves on the love of God. We need to find our worth in him while simultaneously being brutally honest about the good, the bad and the ugly within, knowing it's not about needing to get it right any more. Here, even disappointments can become doorways to fresh encounters with love.

I have found my way to this feast through discovering contemplative spirituality. These ancient ways of praying are being rediscovered across the church as people, looking for fresh water, find it in ancient wells. The willingness to opt for silence, sit in solitude, use structured times and forms of prayer, and meditate on scripture enables us to be sustained by God's constant love. As we stop and take time on our own to focus on God, we can become more mindful of his presence throughout the day. Our stopping anchors us in being not doing. A daily prayer pattern provides a rhythm for keeping in touch with him through the day. Scripture keeps us building on foundations of truth.

To focus in the stillness, I find it helpful to have a short phrase about God that draws me back to him when my mind gets distracted or negative thoughts arise. I use a simplified form of the 'Jesus Prayer' ('Lord Jesus Christ, have mercy on me')[133] or another suitable simple expression, which becomes a repeated phrase throughout my prayer time and one I return to throughout the day. This acts like a metronome, setting the beat for the day and offering a godly, truth-based interior message about who and whose I truly am.

This feasting on the love of God enables us to dwell each day and through each day in that love, which alone will transform us and our false images of God, as well as enabling us eventually to become more compassionate towards ourselves and others.

To rest in the arms of our loving God brings us back into close connection with him. There can be no distance when his arms are wrapped around us and intimacy becomes possible, as we gaze upon love. I used this language with someone recently. 'Ah,' he said, 'it's been a long time since I looked God in the face.'

At the end of a retreat, someone described his experience like this: 'Before, my life was all about my love for God. Now it is about his love for me!' I asked, 'And what has that done for your love for God?' 'Oh, that's indescribable!' he said, as he returned to his life of serving God and others.

Pause to reflect

- Take a few moments to be still with God and enjoy his presence. Allow this taste of love to become the metronome beat of your day.
- George Herbert's poem 'Love (III)', speaks into that concern as to whether we are welcome at this feast. You could use it as a prayer.

Love bade me welcome. Yet my soul drew back
    Guilty of dust and sin.
But quick-eyed Love, observing me grow slack
    From my first entrance in,
Drew nearer to me, sweetly questioning,
    If I lacked any thing.

A guest, I answered, worthy to be here:
    Love said, You shall be he.
I the unkind, ungrateful? Ah my dear,
    I cannot look on thee.
Love took my hand, and smiling did reply,
    Who made the eyes but I?

Truth Lord, but I have marred them: let my shame
    Go where it doth deserve.
And know you not, says Love, who bore the blame?
    My dear, then I will serve.
You must sit down, says Love, and taste my meat:
    So I did sit and eat.[134]

Sharing plate: blessing

Next, we dip into a sharing plate of blessing. Words are more than just words, and the tongue has great power both for good or for ill.

Maurice Berquist tells of the power of blessing. He was once invited to give a short talk preceding the main address by a famous speaker. At the end people crowded around the celebrity to congratulate him, while Berquist began to walk away unnoticed. Then one elderly lady came to him and said, 'Bless you, you gave a wonderful talk. I pray that God will bless your life and make you a blessing to everyone as long as you live. You were a blessing to me today.'[135] Many years later, he still speaks of the huge encouragement her small intervention has been to him. And this is a power that we all have within our grasp. This course is like a sharing platter of delicacies placed in the centre of the table for everyone to enjoy. The gift of blessing flourishes in the midst of community as everyone dips in and shares.

Blessing is deeper and richer than kindly terms of endearment or a handy email sign-off. The Latin equivalent, *benedictio*, from which we get the English 'benediction', literally means speaking well of someone. Blessing is the projection of good into the life of another. It involves words that are loaded with depth of feeling and good will. When Isaac blessed Jacob, the blessing, coming from the depths of his soul, was so powerful that once given it could not be revoked and given to Esau. We need to recover the positive power of blessing.

The opposite of blessing is to diminish rather than to enlarge; to use words, or a lack of them, to tear down rather than build up. We can do this with a raised eyebrow or a shrug of the shoulders. Simply leaving a delay before offering some longed-for positive response can have a devastating impact. And the better you know someone, the easier this is to do.

Like all fine dining, this is one to linger over. To bless or to be blessed cannot be hurried. When someone prays for me after a church service, my awareness of others waiting sometimes makes me anxious not to take up too much time. But in so doing we diminish our receiving. It is worth battling our own sense of unworthiness in order to more fully receive.

God gave this ancient blessing to Moses to be used by his priests:

> The Lord bless you and keep you;
> the Lord make his face to shine upon you, and be gracious
>   to you;
> the Lord lift up his countenance upon you, and give you peace.
> NUMBERS 6:24–26 (NRSV)

These are words of great goodness and divine protection as well as of committed and intimate attention. The blessing incorporates imagery reminiscent of a face alight with love. There is no turning away after a glance nor looking past the person at something beyond; God's countenance is lifted up to make and maintain eye contact and to instil deep peace.

Blessing like this feeds the soul. When were you last deeply encouraged? When did you last take the opportunity to bless? Could you take some time out this week to do so? Can we be intentional in using words that speak goodness rather than harm over the people around us? As we all dip into this sharing plate of blessing, know that it could transform the culture of our churches, communities and more.

Finally, can we dare to speak well to ourselves? Many of the harshest words we speak are to ourselves. A group of leaders were given three minutes to write down all the things they did not like about themselves. The average list numbered 15. They were then given three minutes to list good things about themselves. The average was three; some found none. It's hard to be a blessing when we do not have a positive voice within.

Kristin Neff uses the language of 'self-compassion' to encourage people to speak well to themselves using these steps:

- *Self-kindness* – rather than beating ourselves up, being as warm and understanding towards ourselves when we make a mistake as we would be to others.
- *Common humanity* – recognising that feelings of inadequacy are common to all rather than something that happens to ourselves alone.
- *Mindfulness* – taking a balanced approach to negative emotions so that feelings are neither suppressed nor exaggerated, meaning we are not swept away by negativity.[136]

Self-criticism, like criticism of others, creates a toxic atmosphere within individuals, families, churches and communities. Thankfully, blessing can quickly spread a more pleasing aroma. When we speak well to ourselves, we create a reservoir of blessing that we can extend to others. Everyone gets to dip into the sharing platter.

Pause to reflect

- What words of blessing could you use towards yourself or others this week?
- Charles Stone offers these ways to encourage leaders. Which will you offer?

  - You showed me tangible appreciation, such as a small gift.
  - You let me know that I spiritually impacted your life.
  - You let me know you prayed for me.
  - You accepted and understood me just as I am.
  - You supported my leadership and trusted me.
  - You ministered to my spouse and/or my family.[131]

Side portion: goodness

Since we are being extravagant with this meal, we can afford to order a side portion of goodness.

The apostle Paul wrote:

> You'll do best by filling your minds and meditating on things true, noble, reputable, authentic, compelling, gracious – the best, not the worst; the beautiful, not the ugly; things to praise, not things to curse… Do that, and God… will work you into his most excellent harmonies.
>
> PHILIPPIANS 4:8–9 (MSG)

Paul invites us to feed our lives with things that are truly and deeply good. I'm not advocating a return to puritanical days when the only book which could be read was the Bible, although that is the ultimate good book. Different people will draw their boundaries of truth, authenticity, beauty and goodness in different places, but the key is whether the soul is fed. Here is the invitation to feed ourselves deep nourishment with a day in the countryside or a walk along a beach; to be uplifted by a beautifully written and even challenging book, film or play; to be energised through the exhilaration of live music; or to be inspired by a stroll through an art gallery or a photography exhibition. Ian Cron says, 'The object of all great art is beauty, and it makes us nostalgic for God.'[138]

Pause to reflect

- What have you been feeding on this week?

Wine: intimacy

A good meal is enhanced by fine wine. This represents the intimacy of relationships. We were created for relationship. The first deficiency in creation had nothing to do with forbidden fruit, but was declared when God said, 'It is not good for the man to be alone' (Genesis 2:18). We are made in the image of God and the Trinity is defined by intimate relationship.

Intimacy is about trustful, tender and risky self-disclosure. It requires letting down our walls, manifesting our deeper self to another and allowing the flow to happen. Such vulnerability evokes and allows a reciprocal vulnerability from the other side. However, this is not something that comes naturally, especially for men, who are often torn between the innate desire for intimacy and the fear of baring their soul. In our distorted world, this feels like weakness rather than the strength that it is. We prefer to be invulnerable rather than to live in vulnerability.

Yet people who risk intimacy are invariably happier and more authentic. Their vulnerability forges a mutual connectedness with other people. To avoid intimacy is to be imprisoned in a small and circumscribed world. Intimacy is the gateway into the temple of human and divine love.

I am thankful for those friends I have with whom I can use that word intimacy: friends with whom I have been meeting in a peer support group for 27 years since we trained together; my spiritual director of the last 20 years; and those with whom I have intentionally covenanted to be real. Like the gift of good wine they gladden the soul. Often, we don't spend that much time together. We may be in different churches, have our own roles, belong to different friendship groups or live in different parts of the country. But when we spend precious time together, often over food and drink, we laugh and share openly, build relationship and pray for one another. And when that time is over, my soul feels healthier and perhaps even more intoxicated with passion for the things of God than before we began.

Pause to reflect

- Give thanks for those with whom you share intimate relationship. Ensure you fix up a time to see them soon.
- If it is hard for you to think of someone, consider who you could trust to go further with you on this journey.

Dessert: gratitude

Finally, this feast needs a show-stopping dessert of gratitude, rather than the barren desert of gratitude in which we often live.

Meister Eckhart wrote, 'If the only prayer you say in your entire life is "Thank You", that would suffice.'[139] More recently, Matthieu Ricard, who has been called 'the happiest man in the world', affirmed the power of thanksgiving in a much-viewed TED talk.[140] This wisdom is deeply rooted not only in the Christian faith but also in the wider world of faith and science.

Gratitude is good food for the soul. The *Journal of Happiness Studies* found that participants who wrote three letters of gratitude over a three-week period displayed both increased happiness indicators and decreased symptoms of depression.

Gratitude is powerful because it undoes pride and despair, both of which are poison to the soul. When the disciples returned to Jesus having seen great things happening on mission, rather than focusing on their success, Jesus instructed them to give thanks that their names were written in the book of life (Luke 10:1–20). That is cause for thanksgiving both when much is happening (for which we could be proud) and when nothing is happening (about which we could despair).

Gratitude also punctures our contemporary culture of 'entitlement'. To express thanks is to take something out of the realm of 'a right' and into the realm of 'gift'. Yet thankfulness remains one of the easiest things in the world to forget. In some of the earliest market research ever recorded, we see that nine out of ten lepers forgot to say thank you (Luke 17:17).

Sometimes life is so harsh that we do not know where to begin with thanksgiving. Ignatius of Loyola's advice in such circumstances is 'Start with your next breath.'[141] Try this and see where you end up.

Thanksgiving needs to be intentional. Psychologists tell us that while we instantly and instinctively record disasters, we only remember good things when we deliberately reflect on them for 15 seconds or more. Like Velcro, negative experiences stick, whereas positive ones slide away as if on Teflon. We therefore need to actively hold on to the positive so that it imprints, and is digested by, our soul. Rick Hanson says, 'At the banquets of life, bring a big spoon.'[142]

You can help your brain register positive experiences by keeping a journal of things you're grateful for, sharing three good things each day with a friend or partner, or going out of your way to express gratitude to others.

A tried-and-tested way to partake of this sweet dessert is through the Prayer of Examen, developed by Ignatius of Loyola. This is a prayerful reflection on each day's events through which to notice God's presence and discern his direction for us. We work through these stages:

- *Become aware of God's presence*, looking back on the events of the day in the company of the Holy Spirit.
- *Review the day with gratitude*. Walk through your day with God and note its gifts and joys.
- *Pay attention to emotions*. Reflect on the feelings you experienced. What is God saying through them? As you become aware of ways that you fell short, offer these to God.
- *Ask the Holy Spirit to direct you* to something during the day that is particularly important and pray about it.
- *Look towards tomorrow*. Ask God to give you what you need for tomorrow's challenges.
- *End the Examen* in conversation with Jesus in the spirit of gratitude.

In their book *Sleeping with Bread*, the Linn siblings draw on an image that comes from orphaned children in refugee camps. The children would find it difficult to sleep, fearful that they would wake up to find themselves once again without food. Their carers eventually found that giving each child a piece of bread to hold at bedtime enabled them to sleep in peace. All through the night the bread reminded them, 'Today I ate and I will eat again tomorrow.'[143]

Reflecting with gratitude to God at the end of each day sustains us as we notice God's presence and provision, and readies us to look for them again tomorrow. In its simplest form, the prayer asks two questions: 'For what moment today am I most grateful? For what moment today am I least grateful?' The wonder is that when we learn to feed on gratitude, we become so satiated by it that our lives of thanksgiving overflow into the lives of those who bump into us.

Richard Rohr writes:

> A daily 'attitude of gratitude' keeps your hands open to receive life at ever-deeper levels of satisfaction… Those who live with such open and humble hands receive life's gifts in abundance.[144]

In the film *Arrival* (dir. Denis Villeneuve, 2016), there is an exchange which reveals how the language we use can influence our whole attitude to life. In their attempt to communicate with an alien race we hear this dialogue between the two main characters:

Ian Donnelly:	If you immerse yourself into a foreign language, then you can actually rewire your brain.
Dr Louise Banks:	Yeah, the Sapir-Whorf hypothesis. It's the theory that the language you speak determines how you think and –
Ian Donnelly:	Yeah, it affects how you see everything.

This genuine linguistic hypothesis suggests that to immerse ourselves in the language of thankfulness will come to affect how we view everything. G.K. Chesterton writes:

> You say grace before meals. All right. But I say grace before the concert and the opera, and grace before the play and pantomime, and grace before I open a book, and grace before sketching, painting, swimming, fencing, boxing, walking, playing, dancing and grace before I dip the pen in the ink.[145]

Pause to reflect

- Is there someone you want to send a thank-you note to?
- Would you find it helpful to find time for the daily Examen?

Creating your own menu

This is a menu for feeding your soul with good food. Each course contains its essential ingredients of Bible and prayer as we slow down, rest in God's love, use words of blessing, choose goodness, share intimacy and live lives of thanksgiving. You could use this sample menu as a means of improving your own soul's diet by asking when and how you could partake of these items. What would you want to add to the menu?

Many find it helpful to develop a Rule of Life to offer structure to spiritual disciplines that feed their lives. This provides support for the demanding lives we live in the same way that a vine needs a framework on which to grow.

If you find the language of 'rules' off-putting, you could achieve the same support for your fruitfulness by devising a personal menu of soul food to feed and sustain your life both in the present and into the future.

Set aside some time to make a first attempt at this, then try it out and make adjustments as you find what works for you. Be blessed so that you may be a blessing to others!

HOLDING ON TO HOPE

And so we turn to our onward journey. The sustenance we need will not come from a return to false strength. It must instead originate in something more real and reliable, like hope. But what does hope look like from a place of vulnerability?

Hope is hanging on in there

Sometimes Christian living involves forging ahead to victory. Enjoy those seasons. Other times, simply hanging on as your nails slide painfully down the cliff face is heroic enough. Knowing this releases you from the guilt of feeling we should be doing something more.

Once when God's people faced insurmountable enemies, his specific command was to just hang on in there: 'The battle is not yours, but God's… You will not have to fight… Take up your positions; *stand firm* and see the deliverance the Lord will give you' (2 Chronicles 20:15, 17, emphasis added). That is what happened! The combined enemy armies totally destroyed each other. When the apostle Paul writes of spiritual warfare, the aim is not to advance but simply to stand firm in the armour God supplies (Ephesians 6:10–17). It is a relief to know this is all that is required of us.

A friend shared a traumatic challenge she faced, expressing guilt, failure and inadequacy. She said, 'I feel as if all I am doing is just hanging in there.' But sometimes that's exactly what hope looks like. And hearing that in itself makes the hanging on in there more possible. The apostle Paul writes, 'Waiting does not diminish us, any more than waiting diminishes a pregnant mother. We are enlarged in the waiting' (Romans 8:24, MSG).

I know myself that hanging on in there doesn't feel very heroic. It more often feels like a stumbling lurch from one crisis to another. But somehow people notice our hanging on. A former colleague approached me to offer his thanks. 'Thank you for what?' I replied. 'Thank you for hanging on in there. It has meant so much to me.'

Hope comes from perspective

From one perspective our 2007 family holiday in Montenegro was a total disaster. After an exhausting journey, we found there was no lift to our top-floor apartment, which had no air-conditioning. After carrying our luggage up many flights of steps, we discovered there was no water for a shower, since pressure had been diverted to fight the forest fires blazing nearby. On retiring to bed, we had to deal with a scorpion climbing up the bedroom wall.

Next morning, I swam out to some rocks, but when I reached them, I found they were covered in sea urchins, the spines of which pierced and poisoned my hands and feet. On swimming back to the shore, I noticed my wedding ring had fallen off and lay lost in the rocks many feet below.

From another perspective, however, it was a wonderful holiday. We were together as a family after much stress and exhaustion. We were privileged to be in a beautiful country that was new to us. The apartment offered wonderful views over the Adriatic Sea with fabulous sunsets each evening. The picturesque bay was beautiful and unspoilt. As a family, we drank coffee in ancient town squares, visited World Heritage sights, relaxed together, laughed – even about the disasters – and definitely enjoyed the best pizza we have ever eaten.

Even the bad things had their upside. On seeing us looking for the wedding ring, local people joined our search. The doctor who removed my urchin spines spoke little English, but he had a friend staying with him who spoke perfect English. And not only did the doctor have great skill but also warm hospitality; it remains the only time a visit to a doctor has been accompanied by the offer of an aperitif at ten in the morning!

I can tell the 'Woe is me' version or the 'Wasn't it amazing?' version of that holiday. I know which one of these I naturally tend towards in life, but for that holiday I found it easy to focus on the positive. We still look back on it as one of the best holidays we've ever had.

Sometimes hope is about perspective. I don't know at which end of the spectrum you most naturally find yourself, but I am learning to ask whether I need to move from a 'Woe is me' to an 'Isn't it amazing?' perspective. A human weakness, which makes it harder to maintain perspective, is our tendency to emphasise *either* the extreme negative *or* the totally positive – whereas life is more complex than that.

The animated film *Inside Out* (dir. Pete Docter, Ronnie del Carmen, 2015) portrays the story of a young girl, Riley, from the perspective of the personified emotions that run her life from the inside. Joy, Sadness, Anger, Fear and Disgust compete to take hold of the control panel inside her brain. Initially Joy runs the show and is proud of the pure golden memories that go into Riley's long-term memory. When Sadness touches a memory, it is considered disastrous that the memory is tainted blue. But through their adventure, Joy and Sadness find they have to work together until Riley's memories are no longer pure golden joy or total blue sadness. They become beautifully rainbow-coloured as each emotion takes its place.

Can we too learn to integrate both positives and negatives to enable life's richer tapestry to be revealed and reach a more honest and realistic perspective? Can we embrace a theology that is not toppled by the imperfections of life?

Can we even learn to cope with those times when we lose our experience of the tangible reality of God? God does bless us with the sense of his loving touch upon our lives, but such experiences alone cannot sustain hope in the long run. When I lost the real daily experience of the presence of God for a long time, I did not know at first how to cope with his absence. While embracing times of God's close presence when they came as gifts of grace, I also had to be willing to let go of building too much on them. Instead I am learning to build hope on what God has said to us in his word and what he has already done for us in Jesus.

This isn't to minimise the fact that sometimes bad things happen to good people. I am not encouraging denial or a lack of authenticity. But I am convinced that we will be better able to hold on to hope if we can develop a sense of perspective. Eugene Peterson says:

> Exile always forces a decision: will I focus my attention on what is wrong with the world and feel sorry for myself? Or will I focus my energies on how I can live at my best in this place I find myself?[146]

This is what hope looks like.

Hope does not equal optimism

Hope is *not* the same as optimism. A frequent response to crisis is a cheery, 'I'm sure it will be fine.' However, it may not be fine at all. This response often masks a discomfort with suffering, which is consequently pushed away with a platitude. David Henderson makes this differentiation:

> Optimism claims everything will be all right despite reality. Hope accepts reality as it is... optimism gets ground up by reality, but hope goes toe-to-toe with reality because of a heart that refuses to quit.[147]

Christians can go further to say that hope accepts reality as it is and draws on something deeper – the presence and promises of God.

When the apostle Peter writes to suffering Christians, he doesn't promise that persecution will cease. He has seen and experienced too much suffering for that. Instead of empty optimism, he offers something better – a living hope based on the death and resurrection of Jesus, which opens up the way into an inheritance that is impervious to circumstances (1 Peter 1:3ff).

That doesn't mean it is wrong in the face of trials to hope for healing, peace or resolution. But *what* we hope for is secondary to *who* we hope in. The Psalms frequently express this, saying, 'My hope is in you' (e.g. Psalm 25:5; 39:7).

We all hope God's plan for us will be a straight line from A to B, whereas our experience is more complicated than that. Henri Nouwen says:

> Optimism makes us live as if someday soon things will go better. Hope frees us from the need to predict the future and allows us to live in the present, with the deep trust that God will never leave us alone.[148]

Hope declares that whatever we are facing now or will face in the future, the God who endured the cross and rose again is with us and for us. Even when life doesn't make sense, things go from bad to worse or we feel that we have been abandoned, the deeper truth is that God is not absent from our traumas or disabled by our tragedies. He has a literally awesome capacity to be at work for good when bad things happen along the way.

Hope maintains that the story is not yet complete. A legend of King Solomon tells that he charged his sages to invent a sentence which would be true in all situations. Eventually, they presented him with these words: 'And this, too, shall pass away.'

Here's an illustration of hope from football. In 2001 England played Germany in a World Cup qualifier. I 'hoped' for a rare England win, but when Germany scored after six minutes, my hopes sank. Football fans will remember, however, that something extraordinary happened, as England recovered to eventually win 5–1!

Beforehand, my 'hope' for victory was pure optimism. When Germany scored my hopes sank because I didn't know the end of the story. We often live in that 1–0 moment. Optimistic hope is dented by each negative event or difficult circumstance.

But Christian hope is not like watching the match for the first time, on the edge of our seat. Hope is like me watching the game over again on *Match of the Day*. This time, when Germany scored, I did not panic. My hope of England winning was a sure and certain one based on knowing what the end result was going to be.

Of course, life is more complicated than football. Life gets tough in unexpected and serious ways. But this principle for holding on stands. It is knowing that whatever happens, hope can remain intact because we know the end result. Our trust is determined not by present experience but by our knowledge of how the story will finally end.

Scripture reassures us that our present sufferings bear no comparison with the glory that will be revealed in us. The Spirit is the guarantee that everything God has promised for us will be ours. God's saving work in us will be brought to completion and we will be conformed to the image of his Son. Jesus will return and there will be a new heaven and a new earth in which every tear will be wiped away, doubts will vanish and there will be no more death or crying or pain. God will be so visibly present in the New Jerusalem that he will be our light, as darkness vanishes forever (Romans 8:18, 29; Ephesians 1:14; Philippians 1:6; Revelation 21).

There's a relentlessness about this story in which we have been included, meaning it will reach its end point not interrupted but rather fulfilled by death. Until that story has been completed, hope even in the face of darkness can remain. Brennan Manning says:

> In the end, nothing can harm you permanently; no loss is lasting, no defeat more than transitory, no disappointment is conclusive. Suffering, failure, loneliness, sorrow, discouragement, and death will be part of your journey, but the kingdom of God will conquer all these horrors.[149]

The film *The Best Exotic Marigold Hotel* (dir. John Madden, 2011) includes the line 'Everything will be all right in the end... if it's not all right then it's not yet the end.' Christian hope thus looks the worst that can happen in the face and keeps hold of trust. We experience hope not as an absence of troubles but as the presence of God right where we are. We walk through the valley of the shadow of death and find that the Lord walks with us. We experience weakness and find God's grace is sufficient. We suffer bereavement and encounter the comfort which only God can bring.

We need one another here. Hope is more robust in community than on our own. We need to stand alongside those experiencing darkness and pain. These signs of the kingdom offer us a hope robust enough to hold on to in the face of trials that come in the Lord's service.

In 2007, I thought my ministry story was at an end. I was broken beyond repair and had no idea when or if I would offer any form of ministry again. The pages ahead did not look good. Trusted friends shared that the best was yet to come, but it was too hard to believe at that time.

However, the story had not ended and I am here to share this truth: our hope is not that every part of our story makes perfect sense, but that we remember how our story with God will end. And we experience – sometimes as bright as the noonday sun and sometimes as gently as the dawn breaking at the end of the darkest night – that right where we are, God is with us. We do not need to be afraid. That is hope. The best is indeed yet to come. Richard Rohr writes:

> The Risen Christ is the standing icon of humanity in its final and full destiny. He is the pledge and guarantee of what God will do with all of our crucifixions. At last, we can meaningfully live with hope… Our hurts now become the home for our greatest hopes.[150]

Hope overflows into evangelism

Where does evangelism fit into this message about restoring hope to busy ministers and worn-out servants obediently trying to respond to God's call? It's quite simple. Pope Francis recently tweeted, 'God does not disappoint! He has placed hope in our hearts so that it can blossom and bear fruit.' Evangelism is about sharing good news. And surely real hope is good news worth sharing. It gives us something more powerful to offer the world than some bubble-wrapped experience of life, where nothing bad ever happens. How could we then come alongside those excluded from this privileged existence?

Henri Nouwen says, 'Christian community is the place where we keep the flame of hope alive among us… so that it can grow and become stronger in us.'[151] In being rooted in Christian community we deepen our experience of hope so that when we encounter those whose journeys have taken them to the worst of places, we can meet them there. We can stay with them there and go beyond worldly optimism to speak of a hope that trusts it is not the end of God's story with them. We comfort others with the comfort we ourselves have received from the 'Father of compassion and the God of all comfort' (2 Corinthians 1:3).

We have something to offer that goes beyond the 'everything will be fine' escapism of the world. In life and in death, we have something to say that is based on the facts of the life, death and resurrection of Jesus, which makes a difference in the complex challenges we face in our day-to-day lives.

We live in a world in need of hope. We look at the natural world and the bizarre extremes of climate now occurring across the globe and we know that creation itself groans for hope. The cry comes from people too. Relationships are under pressure. People, often wisely, mistrust authority. Many are lost in materialism and falling prey to addictions. Anger simmers just under the surface. Millions have been impacted by recessions and the widening gap between rich and poor. Food banks respond daily to the effects of systemic injustice. Alienated from God, unsure of their significance and purpose, is it any wonder that people are looking for hope?

And that is what we have to offer. Being church and having hope go together, and it is the Spirit's work to set our hearts ablaze with a hope worth sharing with a hope-hungry world. This will involve both words and deeds. Evangelism in terms of telling the good news spills over into being good news. Augustine of Hippo writes, 'Hope has two beautiful daughters. Their names are anger and courage; anger at the way things are, and courage to see that they do not remain the way they are.'[152] So the hope we have about how things could be becomes a resource for inspiring the anger and the courage needed to do something about injustice within our world.

We finish, then, with this renewed call to the mission field, to our areas of leadership, ministry and service. Remember Elijah, who reached that point of being so emptied of all hope for ministry that he wanted to give up on life itself. God ministered to him, spoke to him and restored him. And then, he sent him right back into the midst of what he had been doing before. He had a task to complete, but having had rest for his body, time out of the crisis and a fresh encounter with the living God, he was ready, willing and able to do just that (1 Kings 19:1–18).

I pray for you who have read this book that your hope too will be restored – hope to hang on in there, because you may need all your energy to do that; hope that goes beyond optimism because it is based on the unfailing promises of God; hope that offers true perspective on the ups and downs of life; and a hope to share in words and deeds with our hope-hungry world.

> May the God of hope fill you with all joy and peace as you trust in him, so that you may overflow with hope by the power of the Holy Spirit.
> ROMANS 15:13

NOTES

1 Parker J. Palmer, *Let Your Life Speak: Listening for the voice of vocation* (Jossey-Bass, 2000), p. 30.

2 David Runcorn, *Space for God: Silence and solitude in the Christian life* (Darton, Longman and Todd, 1990), p. 40.

3 Revd Mark Oakley, Canon Chancellor of St Paul's Cathedral, London, speaking at the National Conference for Diocesan Spirituality Advisers, March 2014.

4 Sheila Cassidy, quoted in Chris Morley, *Caring Together: A study guide* (Kevin Mayhew, 2011), p. 14.

5 Russ Parker, *Free to Fail* (Triangle Books, 1998), p. vii.

6 The phrase 'dark night of the soul' is drawn from the poem of the same name by the 16th-century Spanish mystic John of the Cross.

7 Haruki Murakami, *Kafka on the Shore* (Vintage, 2006), p. 4.

8 Richard Rohr, *Adam's Return: The five promises of male initiation* (Independent Publishers Group, 2004), p. 40.

9 Caroline Phelps, 'Voices', talk at Trinity Cheltenham, 26 October 2014, **trinitycheltenham.com/Podcasts/voices-caroline-phelps-pm**.

10 Henri J.M. Nouwen, *The Inner Voice of Love: A journey through anguish to freedom* (Doubleday, 1998), p. 5.

11 Clare of Assisi, from her letters, quoted at Life of the Saints, **piercedhearts.org/theology_heart/life_saints/clare_assisi.htm**.

12 Sir Jonathan Sacks, former Chief Rabbi of the UK, **rabbisacks.org/covenant-conversation-5768-behaalotcha-humility**

13 Eugene Peterson, 'Living into God's story', **biblicaltheology.ca/blue_files/Living%20into%20God%27s%20Story.pdf**.

14 Harold S. Kushner, *When Bad Things Happen to Good People* (Pan, 2002), p. 128.

15 Chris Russell, *Ten Letters* (Darton, Longman and Todd, 2012), p. 115.

16 Mike Bickle, 'Leaning on our beloved', 11 March 2000, **mikebickle.org/resources/series/leaning-on-our-beloved**.

17 Justin Welby quoted in an interview with Charles Moore, *The Daily Telegraph*, 23 November 2017.

18 Richard Rohr, 'Intimacy: The divine ambush', conference presentation in Santa Fe, New Mexico, April 2013. Audio file available at **store.cac.org/Intimacy-The-Divine-Ambush-MP3_p_303.html**.

19 Pierre Teilhard de Chardin, S.J., 'Patient trust', in Michael Harter, S.J. (ed.), *Hearts on Fire: Praying with Jesuits* (Chestnut Hill, MA: Institute of Jesuit Sources, 1993), p. 58. Reproduced with permission.

20 Revd Canon J. John introducing himself at a conference on evangelism in Malvern, Worcestershire, 2004.

21 Brendan Busse, 'Andrew Garfield played a Jesuit in *Silence*, but he didn't expect to fall in love with Jesus', *America: The Jesuit review*, 23 January 2017.

22 John Holmes, *When I Am Weak* (Darton, Longman and Todd, 1992), p. 1.

23 Brené Brown, *The Gifts of Imperfection: Let go of who you think you're supposed to be and embrace who you are* (Hazelden, 2010), pp. 16, 26.

24 E.E. Cummings, 'A poet's advice to students', *The Journal of Humanistic Psychology*, 1 October 1972.

25 Konstantin Stanislavski, quoted in Alison Siewert, *Drama Team Handbook* (InterVarsity Press, 2003), p. 92.

26 This reflection from Joe Vorstermans is an extract from an email from Henri Nouwen Society, 'Daily E-Meditation', **henrinouwen.org/ resources/daily-meditation**. I no longer have the email and at the time of writing the archive link on the website was not working.

27 Jean Vanier, *Community and Growth* (Paulist Press, 1989), p. 185.

28 Luther's (and in turn Lutheran) theology of *simul justus et peccator* emerged from his thinking that since Christ and the believer hold all things in common, they are both righteous and sinners at the same time. See *Luther's Works Volume 31: Career of the Reformer 1* (Augsburg Fortress Press, 1959), pp. 351–53.

29 Joseph Cooke, quoted in Dwight K. Nelson, *The Chosen: God's Dream for You* (Review and Herald Publishing, 2011), p. 203.

30 Rowan Williams, *Silence and Honey Cakes: The wisdom of the desert* (Lion, 2004), p. 47.

31 Williams, *Silence and Honey Cakes*, p. 51.

32 Costica Bradatan, 'Failure happens to everyone – but to grow, you must learn how to turn it into humility', *Quartz*, 5 July 2017, **qz.com/1021499/everyone-fails-but-only-the-wise-find-humility**.

33 Ian Morgan Cron, *Chasing Francis: A pilgrim's tale* (Zondervan 2013), p. 70.

34 Richard Rohr, *Immortal Diamond: The search for our true self* (SPCK, 2013), p. xxi. Emphasis added.

35 Brennan Manning, *The Signature of Jesus: Living a life of holy passion and unreasonable faith* (Multnomah Press, 2004), p. 14.

36 Church of England Morning Prayer, Christmas Season (Church House Publishing), **churchofengland.org/prayer-and-worship/worship-texts-and-resources/common-worship/daily-prayer/morning-and-evening#mm008e7c**.

37 Paula Gooder, *Journey to the Manger: Exploring the birth of Jesus* (Canterbury Press, 2015), p xiii.

38 Richard Rohr with Mike Morrell, *The Divine Dance: The Trinity and your transformation* (Whitaker House, 2016), p. 59.

39 Henri J.M. Nouwen, 'Being broken', 15 July 2017, **henrinouwen.org/mediation/being-broken**.

40 Joseph F. Schmidt, *Everything Is Grace: The life and way of Thérèse of Lisieux* (The Word Among Us Press, 2007), p. 21.

41 'American idols: Larry Crabb says there's something better than control and success', *Christianity Today*, summer 2004, **christianitytoday.com/pastors/2004/summer/8.24.html**.

42 Richard Rohr, *Falling Upward: A spirituality for the two halves of life* (Jossey-Bass, 2011), p. xxii.

43 Brené Brown, *Daring Greatly: How the courage to be vulnerable transforms the way we live, love, parent, and lead* (Portfolio Penguin, 2013), p. 34.

44 Brennan Manning, *The Ragamuffin Gospel* (Multnomah Press 2005), p. 192.

45 Parker J. Palmer, 'Faith or Frenzy: Living contemplation in a world of action', speech at Trinity United Methodist Church, 1992.

46 Charles Spurgeon, quoted in Jim Elliff, 'Hard Work: The Spurgeon way', **ccwtoday.org/2008/04/hard-work-the-spurgeon-way**.

47 J.R.R. Tolkien, *The Fellowship of the Ring* (Mariner Books, 2012), p. 32.

48 Kate Rugani, 'Self-care is not self-ish', 13 August 2012, **faithandleadership.com/self-care-not-self-ish**.

49 Rugani, 'Self-care is not self-ish'.

50 Jeanette Hicks, quoted in Rugani, 'Self-care is not self-ish'.

51 Reported in Kate Rugani, 'Those who flourish in ministry are intentional about their well-being', 21 February 2017, **faithandleadership.com/those-who-flourish-ministry-are-intentional-about-their-well-being**.

52 Brown, *The Gifts of Imperfection*, p. 87.

53 Rae Jean Proeschold-Bell, quoted in Rugani, 'Those who flourish in ministry are intentional about their well-being'.

54 Palmer, *Let Your Life Speak*, p. 30.

55 Robert McAllister, quoted in Andrew Irvine, *Between Two Worlds: Understanding and managing clergy stress* (Mowbray, 1997), p. 28.

56 John Ortberg, *Soul Keeping: Caring for the most important part of you* (Zondervan, 2014), p. 23.

57 Richard Rohr, *What the Mystics Know: Seven pathways to your deeper self* (Crossroad Publishing Company, 2015), p. 83.

58 James Joyce, *A Painful Case*, **online-literature.com/james_joyce/964**.

59 St Augustine, *Confessions* (Oxford University Press, 1991), p. 209.

60 Paulo Coelho, *Veronika Decides to Die* (HarperCollins, 2014), p. 67.

61 From email correspondence, reproduced with permission.

62 Brown, *The Gifts of Imperfection*, p. 83.

63 Henri J.M. Nouwen, *The Return of the Prodigal Son: A story of homecoming* (Darton, Longman and Todd, 1994), p. 127.

64 Stephen Verney, *Water into Wine: An introduction to John's gospel* (Fount Paperbacks, 1985), p. 109.

65 Liz Guthridge, 'How are you being?', 12 January 2015, **connectconsultinggroup.com/how-are-you-being**.

66 Guthridge, 'How are you being?'

67 Brown, *The Gifts of Imperfection*, pp. 10–11.

68 Victor Lipman, 'All successful leaders need this quality: self-awareness', *Forbes*, 18 November 2013.

69 Sheila Walsh, quoted in Peter Scazzero, *Emotionally Healthy Spirituality: Unleash a revolution in your life in Christ* (Thomas Nelson, 2006), p. 79.

70 Scazzero, *Emotionally Healthy Spirituality*, p. 15ff.

71 Quoted in Scazzero, *Emotionally Healthy Spirituality*, p. 23.

72 Augustine of Hippo, quoted in Scazzero, *Emotionally Healthy Spirituality*, p. 65.

73 Dan Allender and Tremper Longman, quoted in Scazzero, *Emotionally Healthy Spirituality*, p. 74.

74 Scazzero, *Emotionally Healthy Spirituality*, p. 75ff.

75 Thomas Merton, quoted in Rohr, *Falling Upward*, p. xvii.

76 Stephen Levine, quoted in Rohr, *Immortal Diamond*, p. 34.

77 Sheila Walsh, quoted in Scazzero, *Emotionally Healthy Spirituality*, p. 80.

78 Teresa of Avila, quoted in Joseph F. Sica, *Embracing Change: 10 ways*

to grow spiritually and emotionally (Twenty-Third Publications, 2003), p. 9.

79 David G.R. Keller, *Oasis of Wisdom: The worlds of the desert fathers and mothers* (Liturgical Press, 2005), p. 143.

80 Ian Morgan Cron and Suzanne Stabile, *The Road Back to You Study Guide* (Inter-Varsity Press, 2016), p. 13.

81 Tessi Rickabaugh, 'The search for deep honesty', 12 January 2017, **sdiworld.org/blog/search-deep-honesty**.

82 Understanding your personality type is valuable, but isn't always as simple as doing a questionnaire. A combination of study, test, consultation and feedback is recommended. For information on Myers Briggs see **myersbriggs.org**, with a list of practicioners at **bapt.org.uk/type-practitioners**. I used **insightsforchange.co.uk**. For Enneagram testing and information see **typologypodcast.com**.

83 Rabbi Zusya, quoted in Martin Buber, *Tales of the Hassidim: The early masters* (Shocken Books, 1968), p. 141.

84 Rohr, *Immortal Diamond*, p. 10.

85 Justin Welby, 'A personal statement from the Archbishop of Canterbury', 8 April 2016, **archbishopofcanterbury.org/speaking-and-writing/articles/personal-statement-archbishop-canterbury**.

86 Rohr, *Immortal Diamond*, p. 14.

87 For a discussion on attribution see **quoteinvestigator.com/2014/01/20/be-yourself**.

88 Henri J.M. Nouwen, *Life of the Beloved* (Hodder and Stoughton, 1992), p. 26. See also Brennan Manning, *Abba's Child: The cry of the heart for intimate belonging* (NavPress, 2015), p. 32.

89 Niels Bohr, quoted in Karen Barad, *Meeting the Universe Halfway: Quantum physics and the entanglement of matter and meaning* (Duke University Press, 2007), p. 254.

90 Jody Cross, 'Teach me to abide', 22 March 2016, **sharpeningleaders.com/to-the-point/teach-me-to-abide**.

91 Brown, *The Gifts of Imperfection*, p. 34.

92 Julian of Norwich, *Showings*, chapter 22 (short text), trans. Edmund Colledge and James Walsh (Paulist Press, 1978), p. 164.

93 Nouwen, *The Return of the Prodigal Son*, p. 128.

94 Margery Kempe, quoted in Manning, *The Ragamuffin Gospel*, p 120.

95 Brennan Manning, *The Relentless Tenderness of Jesus* (Revell, 2004), p. 120.

96 Sheridan Voysey, *Unseen Footprints Study Guide* (Discovery House, 2011/2016), p. 19.

97 Walter Brueggemann, *Theology of the Old Testament: Testimony, dispute, advocacy* (Fortress, 1997), p. 216.

98 Richard Rohr, *Adult Christianity and How to Get There*, CD (CAC, 2004), disc 1.

99 Edwina Gateley, *Psalms of a Laywoman* (Anthony Clarke, 1986), p. 49. Reproduced with permission.

100 Edwina Gateley, *I Hear a Seed Growing* (Orbis Books, 2010), p. 203. Reproduced with permission.

101 Meyer Friedman, quoted in John Ortberg, *The Life You've Always Wanted* (Zondervan, 2002), p. 78.

102 Lewis Carroll, *Alice's Adventures in Wonderland and Through the Looking-Glass* (Cosimo Classics, 2010), p. 20.

103 Peter Scazzero and Warren Bird, *The Emotionally Healthy Church: A strategy for discipleship that actually changes lives* (Zondervan, 2013), p. 26.

104 Scazzero, *Emotionally Healthy Spirituality*, pp. 31, 34.

105 Brené Brown, '3 ways to set boundaries', *Huffington Post*, 12 September 2013, **huffingtonpost.com/2013/12/09/how-to-set-boundaries-brene-brown_n_4372968.html**.

106 Brown, '3 ways to set boundaries'.

107 Karl Vaters, 'Epidemic: Another pastor burned out and quit last Sunday', *Christianity Today*, September 2016, **christianitytoday.com/karl-vaters/2016/september/epidemic-another-pastor-burned-out-and-quit-last-sunday.html**.

108 Benjamin Hoff, *The Tao of Pooh* (Penguin Books, 1982), p. 101.

109 Richard J. Krejcir, 'Statistics on pastors: 2016 update', **files.stablerack.com/webfiles/71795/pastorsstatWP2016.pdf**.

110 Richard J. Krejcir, 'Church leadership statistics on pastors', **churchleadership.org/apps/articles/default.asp?articleid=42347**.

111 Krejcir, 'Statistics on pastors: 2016 update'.

112 Yvonne Warren, quoted in 'Causes of clergy stress aired in the General Synod', *The Church Times*, 9 July 2017, **churchtimes.co.uk/articles/2017/7-july/news/uk/causes-of-clergy-stress-aired-in-the-general-synod**.

113 'I was pushed close to the edge', *The Church Times*, 13 October 2017, **churchtimes.co.uk/articles/2017/13-october/features/features/i-was-pushed-close-to-the-edge**.

114 Sherrie Bourg Carter, 'The tell tale signs of burnout... do you have them?', *Psychology Today*, 26 November 2013, **psychologytoday.com/blog/high-octane-women/201311/the-tell-tale-signs-burnout-do-you-have-them**.

115 Margery Williams, *The Velveteen Rabbit* (Little Mammoth, 1992), pp. 8–9.

116 Bruce Springsteen, *Born to Run* (Simon and Schuster, 2017), p. 271.

117 Quoted in Mohan Doss, *Led by the Spirit: Mission, spirituality and formation* (DWS/ISPCK, 2008), p. 136. See also **usccb.org/prayer-and-worship/prayers-and-devotions/prayers/prophets-of-a-future-not-our-own.cfm**.

118 Walter Brueggemann, *Sabbath as Resistance: Saying no to the culture of now* (Westminster John Knox Press, 2014), p. xiii.

119 Brueggemann, *Sabbath as Resistance*, p. 40.

120 Susie Steiner, 'Top five regrets of the dying', *The Guardian*, 1 February 2012, **theguardian.com/lifeandstyle/2012/feb/01/top-five-regrets-of-the-dying**.

121 Vincent de Paul, quoted in Tony Horsfall, *Rhythms of Grace: Finding intimacy with God in a busy life* (Kingsway 2004), p. 46.

122 Stephen R. Covey, *The 7 Habits of Highly Effective People* (Franklin Covey, 2013), p. 78.

123 Marva J. Dawn, *The Sense of the Call: A sabbath way of life* (Eerdmans, 2006), p. 35.

124 Marva J. Dawn, *Keeping the Sabbath Wholly: Ceasing, resting, embracing, feasting* (Eerdmans, 1989).

125 'Aesop and the bow', in *Aesop's Fables*, translated by Laura Gibb (Oxford University Press, 2008). See also **mythfolklore.net/aesopica/oxford/537.htm**.

126 Tony Horsfall, *Working from a Place of Rest: Jesus and the key to sustaining ministry* (BRF, 2010), p. 60.

127 Eugene Peterson, *The Contemplative Pastor: Returning to the art of spiritual direction* (Eerdmans, 1989), p. 168.

128 Skye Jethani, 'Limping leaders: for a generation fixated on sprinting, failure is producing a better way', *Christianity Today*, March 2005, **christianitytoday.com/pastors/2005/march-online-only/cln50314.html**.

129 Ortberg, *Soul Keeping*, p. 20.

130 Rachel Cooke, 'Marco Pierre White: My work was a painkiller – it was where I hid', *The Observer*, 18 January 2015, **theguardian.com/lifeandstyle/2015/jan/18/sp-marco-pierre-white-my-work-was-a-painkiller**.

131 Monica Furlong, extract from *The Parson's Role Today*, a paper given at the Wakefield Diocesan Clergy Conference, April 1966.

132 Martin Laird, *Into the Silent Land: The practice of contemplation* (Dartman, Longman and Todd, 2006), p. 9.

133 The prayer in full is 'Lord Jesus Christ, Son of God, have mercy upon me, a sinner.'

134 George Herbert, 'Love III', first published in George Herbert, *The Temple* (1633), **poetryfoundation.org/poems/44367/love-iii**

135 Maurice Berquist, *The Miracle and the Power of Blessing*, **twolisteners.org/wp-content/uploads/2017/07/MiracleAndPowerOfBlessing.pdf**.

136 See Kristin Neff, *Self-Compassion: The proven power of being kind to yourself* (William Morrow and Company, 2015), p. 41ff.

137 Adapted from Charles Stone, 'Six ways to encourage your pastor', **charlesstone.com/six-ways-to-encourage-your-pastor**.

138 Cron, *Chasing Francis*, p. 109.

139 August Turak, 'A leadership lesson from Meister Eckhart', *Forbes*, 5 August 2011, **forbes.com/sites/augustturak/2011/08/05/a-leadership-lesson-from-meister-eckhart/#238dc70a6c40**.

140 Matthieu Ricard, 'The habits of happiness', TED2004, February 2004, **ted.com/talks/matthieu_ricard_on_the_habits_of_happiness**.

141 'An Ignatian way to live', **jesuit.org.uk/ignatian-way-live**.

142 Rick Hanson, 'Taking in the good', **rickhanson.net**.

143 Dennis Linn, Sheila Fabricant Linn and Matthew Linn, *Sleeping with Bread: Holding what gives you life* (Paulist Press, 1995), p. 1.

144 Richard Rohr, *Breathing under Water: Spirituality and the twelve steps* (SPCK, 2016), p. 65.

145 G.K. Chesterton, quoted in Katherine Gibson, *Pause: Putting the brakes on a runaway life* (Insomniac Press, 2014), p. 39.

146 Eugene H. Peterson, *Run with the Horses: The quest for life at its best* (IVP, 2009), p. 151.

147 David Henderson, 'Optimism vs hope', 16 January 2013, **couragerenewal.org/optimism-vs-hope**.

148 Henri J.M. Nouwen, *Here and Now: Living in the Spirit* (Crossroad, 1994), p. 33.

149 Manning, *The Relentless Tenderness of Jesus*, p. 182.

150 Rohr, *Immortal Diamond*, p. 84.

151 Henri J.M. Nouwen, *Finding My Way Home: Pathways to life and the Spirit* (Darton, Longman and Todd, 2001), p. 98.

152 Augustine of Hippo, quoted by Robert McAfee Brown, *Spirituality and Liberation: Overcoming the great fallacy* (Westminster John Knox Press, 1988), p. 136.

GUIDELINES

BIBLE STUDY FOR TODAY'S MINISTRY AND MISSION

Guidelines is for people who are hungry for deeper study, who are ready to hear what current biblical scholarship has to say and what differing theological viewpoints may exist, and who want to make up their own mind on how the passage becomes relevant for them.

Available in print (at £4.50 per copy, with free postage when ordered in a group), as an app for Android, iPhone and iPad, and also as a downloadable PDF.

Visit **biblereadingnotes.org.uk** to order your sample copy!

BRF

Transforming
lives and communities

Christian growth and understanding of the Bible

Resourcing individuals, groups and leaders in churches for their
own spiritual journey and for their ministry

Church outreach in the local community

Offering three programmes that churches are embracing
to great effect as they seek to engage
with their local communities
and transform lives

Teaching Christianity in primary schools

Working with children and teachers to explore Christianity
creatively and confidently

Children's and family ministry

Working with churches and families to explore Christianity
creatively and bring the Bible alive

Visit **brf.org.uk** for more information on BRF's work

brf.org.uk

The Bible Reading Fellowship (BRF) is a Registered Charity (No. 233280)